HH IS THE RIGHT MAN FOR ZAMBIA
And Other Acclaimed Articles on Zambia and Africa

CHARLES MWEWA

2021

Copyright © 2021 Charles Mwewa

PUBLISHED BY:

Africa in Canada Press (ACP)

Ottawa, Canada

All rights reserved.

ISBN: 978-1-988251-52-3

DEDICATION

For His Excellency, Hakainde Hichilema,
7th President of the Republic of Zambia.

CONTENTS

DEDICATION	iii
CONTENTS	v
ACKNOWLEDGMENTS	ix
INTRODUCTION	1
1 ZAMBIA: 2021, ELECT HH FOR GOOD REASONS	7
2 HH IS THE RIGHT MAN FOR THE JOB	9
3 THE WAR ZAMBIA MUST FIGHT AND WIN	13
4 A THOUSAND THOUGHTS FOR ZAMBIA	19
5 ZAMBIA IS NOT A PROVINCE IN NIGERIA	21
6 ZAMBIA – COMPARED TO ONTARIO & SWITZERLAND	23
7 THE 30-60-10 UPPER-INCOME ECONOMIC THEORY	25
8 UNJUSTIFIED POVERTY IN ZAMBIA	29
Good Institutions but Still Poor	30
Reversal of Fortunes	31
The Curse of Mineral Resources	33
The HIV/AIDS Excuse	34
No Political Instability but Still Poor	35
Disease Does Not Cause Poverty	35
Zambian Culture Does Not Promote Poverty	36
Real Action is Required	37
9 DOMICILITY CLAUSE	39
10 TEN REASONS WHY DUAL CITIZENSHIP IS GOOD	

FOR ZAMBIA	43
11 WILL ZAMBIA BECOME A MATURE DEMOCRACY?	53
12 THE UGLY ONES ARE DYING BUT THE BEAUTIFUL ONES ARE STILL NOT YET BORN	57
13 LET JUSTICE BE DONE THOUGH THE HEAVENS FALL	61
14 MUGABE-KIBAKI SIGNATURE	67
In Search of a Political Culture	68
Democratic-Minded Leadership	69
Benchmarks for Democratic Progress	70
Emerging African Leadership	72
15 MUGABE: HEARTLESS DEMAGOGUE OR CREATURE OF IMPERIAL AVARICE?	73
Which View?	73
The Western View of Mugabe	74
The Real Issue	74
Westphalian Model	76
Africa Should Learn to Read between the Lines	76
African Ubuntu is Anti-Xenophobia	77
16 GENOCIDE IN DARFUR	79
Tear of God	80
Responsibility to Protect	81
Omar al-Bashir	85
The Right Response	86
17 ALIENOPHOBIA:	89
A CHALLENGE TO CIVILIZED NATIONS	89
18 XENOPHOBIA: HAPPENING IN SOUTH AFRICA	91

19 OMS RULE IN CHINA	93
- AFRICA SHOULD BE WORRIED	93
20 TOOLS OF COLONIALISM: NAMES AND LANGUAGE	97
21 TOOLS OF COLONIALISM: STANDARDS	101
22 OBAMA: LONG WALK TO BLACK POWER	107
From Selma to Montgomery	108
I have been to the Mountaintop	109
The Hands that Built America will Now Rule America	111
Unorthodox Means of Victory	112
Lesson for Zambia's Electoral Process	112
Benedictions	114
23 BARACK OBAMA: TRIUMPH OVER CYNICISM	115
24 END OF RULE BY POLITICIANS – DID BORIS JOHNSON DUPE THE QUEEN?	117
1. Because Politicians have, hitherto, Circumvented the Law	117
2. Because Abuses of Power have, hitherto, been Cloaked in Divided Court Decisions	118
3. Because Even the Queen could be Misled	119
25 ARE EVANGELICALS GAINING THE WORLD AND LOSING THEIR OWN SOULS?	121
Rising Moral Turpitude in the Age of Trump	121
Evangelical Secularism	122
Corruption Unrestrained	123
26 AFROPOSITIVE	125
27 PREACHING AND THE COVID-19 PANDEMIC	127

28 NOT THE TIME TO OPEN CHURCHES	135
29 PRESIDENTIAL LEADERSHIP IN PANDEMIC TIMES	139
Judgment	140
National Coordination (Mobilization/cooperation)	140
Responsible Use of Emergency Powers	140
30 POST-COVID-19 AFRICAN ERA	141
Introduction	141
African Future in a Post-Covid-19 World	153
Western Apathy towards Africa during Covid-19 and Vaccine Distribution Process	154
Africa Must not Only Look to the West for Leadership but within Itself	157
African Governments Must Recruit Raw Talents Scattered Abroad	158
Conclusion	160
ABOUT THE AUTHOR	161
AUTHOR'S CONTACT	163
INDEX	165

ACKNOWLEDGMENTS

To the following Zambian online newspapers (in no particular order):

The Zambian Eye; The Lusaka Times; The Mast; The Zambian Watchdog; The Zambian Reports.

To the African mailers: *The African Executive*; and the *Zimbabwean Chronicles.*

To the Western online media: The *Toronto Pride*; and *Pambazuka.*

To all these news breakers, thank you for publishing my articles or poems across the years.

INTRODUCTION

Hakainde Hichilema (HH) was born on June 4th, 1962. He is Zambia's seventh president after Kenneth Kaunda (UNIP),[1] Frederick Chiluba (MMD),[2] Levy Mwanawasa (MMD), Rupiah Banda (MMD), Michael Sata (PF),[3] and Edgar Lungu (PF). He is the first president to have been elected from the United Party for National Development (UPND) and from outside of the Northern-Luapula-Eastern-Central province enclosure. In this regard, his election on August 12th, 2021 and swearing-in ceremony on August 24th, 2021, were historic. What is not historic is Zambia's over 50 years of tested democratic political power transition tradition. All the six presidents before him handed over power to the in-coming administration peacefully and without any major incidents irrespective of political party background.

African politics have shown that the longer a political party remains in power, the more corrupt it gets. Most of thinking and developmental work and policies are done in the first three years of governing. Once the president and their party become comfortable in power, they begin to slow down and to engineer political machinations. That is why I wrote in an article, thus, "If Zambia gives the PF another five years (it does not make me happy to state the obvious), I will be writing again at this forum of the rampant corruption, poverty and disregard for rule of law that will

---

[1] United National Independence Party (UNIP)
[2] Movement for Multiparty Democracy (MMD)
[3] Patriotic Front (PF)

follow. Lungu and the PF will be emboldened to go full throttle to damage anything and everything in their way."[4]

The purpose of compiling this book is not only the celebration of democracy and the election of HH, but also to demonstrate how prescient my articles on Zambian politics have been during the past over 14 years. Since I immigrated to Canada in 2004, I have neither forgotten about Zambia nor stopped contributing to its political process via newspaper articles and books.[5] This spirit is captured in one of my articles, "A Thousand Thoughts for Zambia."[6] I have spent almost an equal number of years in Africa as in the West. I have the first-hand knowledge and understanding of the issues that captivate the West, and because I have followed African events and politics all these years, I have remained relevant and conversant with global affairs. My research has informed me that Africa (including Zambia) is as blessed and capable of self-government and development as the West. I believe that Zambia shall be the first developed country in Africa. For this reason, I have had keen interest in who rules the nation at any particular point in time.

I believed in HH from the moment he inherited UPND from Anderson Mazoka. I reviewed UPND's platform and manifesto and I listened intently to HH's vision and love for Zambia. Indeed, HH is still the man for Zambia.[7] He means well for the poor and for the image of Zambia at home and abroad.

But it is not a secret that HH has inherited a sinking ship: "Zambian President Hichilema inherits 'empty treasury.'

---

[4] See Chapter 1 of this book
[5] I also served as president for the Zambian-Canadian Foundation from 2009 to 2016, and as Vice-person from 2006 to 2009.
[6] See Chapter 2 of this book
[7] See Chapter 2, *ibid*.

Zambia's new president has told the BBC that he has inherited an 'empty' treasury, while 'horrifying' amounts of money had been stolen. 'People are still trying to make last-minute movements of funds, which are unauthorized, which are not theirs,' President Hakainde Hichilema said."[8] Of course, an 'empty treasury' does not define the wealth of any nation, however, the inference is taken. Zambia needs a manager and visionary leader in HH.

As I have argued in many articles I have written, any president who spends time laundering the indignities of the previous regime, is wasting valuable time to rule. New governments should not be spending the first months in power undoing the contracts of the previous regimes, either, unless it is obvious that those contracts were acquired fraudulently and corruptly. Rather, the new government should continue where the previous administration ended – resources are already thin, if the new government continues from its predecessor's, it stands a better chance to succeed in its policy crafting and implementation. That is one ideal thing Western democracies have never violated.[9]

Every governing party or president, no matter how bad or corrupt they were, did something good for the country. In Zambia, for example, Kenneth Kaunda (KK) established the foundation of the nation and built some notable infrastructure. KK also adopted the idea of *Tribal Balancing* of his Cabinet choice. I submit that HH follows this practice as his opposers may already have cried, "Tribalist," and will be looking for any lapses on the president's part. Frederick Chiluba (FTJ) brought multiparty democracy to Zambia. Levy Mwanawasa and Michael Sata fought corruption.

---

[8] https://www.bbc.com/news/world-africa-58408951 (accessed on September 6th, 2021)
[9] Except, of course, President Trump, and the world watched how his regime ended.

Rupiah Banda willingly allowed the wheels of democracy to move smoothly, even when he had the means to extend his rule contemptibly. And Edgar Lungu has overseen and brought the nation into some form of economic stability (though, with no major pluses for the majority). HH should learn and build on these successes.

HH is now elected. He should rule. The ideas I have written about throughout the past over 14 years stand for the same proposition. And this is the reason why the articles compiled in this book have not been modified. The reader is called on to understand the time and context under which the article was first written.[10]

Living abroad does not absorb us of the "African feeling" – it is our land; we see things from a broader view and perspective, and that is why governments and individuals should take our ideas and writings seriously. We are affected when things don't go well "back home." We are as much its diaspora as its unofficial diplomats.[11] Somewhere, I have advised that those of us in the diaspora are better suited to advancing the interests of governance and development in Africa. The reason is simple: We know the difference and we are part of the two-world formation. It is not because we are double-dipping; our cups are already full in the West.[12] HH should consider erasing the "Domicility Clause" from the *Constitution* to enable its dual citizens in the diaspora to vie for presidential elections. This will enrich the nation with viable and vital national development ideas so that Zambia can become the first country in Africa to be truly developed.[13]

---

[10] Although events might have overtaken the original writing, the principles have remained the same.
[11] See Chapter 5 of this book
[12] See chapters 9 and 10 of this book
[13] See Chapter 7 of this book

Zambia under HH must consider prioritizing the economy, in this sequence: First, embarking on massive legislative enactments to open up the economy for business, promoting small and medium-sized enterprises, deregulating entrepreneurship. This will boost the economy and release the population to have ready access to capital within a favorably deregulated environment.

Second, provide growth incentives to corporations and big companies to create private jobs in all sectors.

And third, launch a universal basic education and healthcare system. This is important given the challenges of Covid-19 and the attendant shortages of vaccines. African nations, in general, have been bogged down with disparities in the distribution of the vaccines by Western-based and barked vaccine producers.[14] At the time I wrote the article entitled, "Genocide in Darfur,"[15] H1N1 was ravaging the world and the suggestions I gave cannot be too true in the Covid-19 pandemic times.

Zambia should begin to recruit talents from the diaspora to serve in various portfolios in government. The synergy this will engender is invaluable to the goal of becoming a developed African economy, breaking the back of poverty permanently.

As stated, this book is the first compilation of the many articles I have written over a period of more than 14 years. They are all already published articles in various online newspapers from Canada, Europe, USA, and Africa and Zambia. The original content has been preserved to retain its historical efficacy and effectuate its contemporary relevance. It is expected that many other volumes will follow.

---

[14] See chapters 16, 27 to 30 of this book
[15] See Chapter 16

Charles Mwewa
Ottawa, Canada
September 2021

1 ZAMBIA: 2021, ELECT HH FOR GOOD REASONS

[Published: February 27th, 2021, *Lusaka Times*]

African politics, Zambia, included, have two political weaknesses; they attack people and neglect issues, and they are rooted in politics of tribe or clan or race or group synergy. This, however, has also been the weakest link to progress and real development. The result has been electing true dunderhead, riffraff and politically malnutritional idea minds. Each five years, Zambia put a "head" at the helm of the "state." But this head is as brainless as the uncertain future it espouses. The outcomes have been obvious: More corruption, more poverty and more undemocratic tendencies. The cows become fat, and the rats rot!

In 2021, Zambia should do everything to elect HH. HH is not a saint, and I don't believe that he is charismatic enough to move millions to elect him. But HH is critically better than Edgar Lungu. For one, Lungu is a president of convenience; you need people like Lungu in power when you run out of ideas or when an incumbent dies without properly naming or grooming a successor. Given five more years, Lungu will lead Zambia into hell – unspeakable poverty, uncontrollable corruption and blatant disregard for democratic institutions and traditions. He has no gravitas to be a dictator – but he has the wisdom to be a soft one. And that is where the problem lies; he cannot control the minions that galvanize his already confused policies, and he cannot discipline the sycophants. He is left to be a *de facto* figurehead and an indecisive ruler.

HH, on the other hand, will not be any different from any other presidents before him, but he will be better: He will do less damage in the first five years of his office – because in Zambia, like in Africa, first always wins. He will be fresh, and therefore, he will be more willing to help the people, at least, before he becomes corrupted like any presidents before him. Give him credit – he has endured all, failed many times but he has decided to hang in there. If not for anything, Zambia must not disregard a leader who has endurance. He is better placed to fight corruption, poverty and democratic failures – at least in comparison to President Lungu.

If Zambia gives the PF another five years (it does not make me happy to state the obvious), I will be writing again at this forum of the rampant corruption, poverty and disregard for rule of law that will follow. Lungu and the PF will be emboldened to go full throttle to damage anything and everything in their way. They will get richer (at least PF worshippers) and the people of Zambia will feed on more and more lies, while reaping more poverty and more disillusionment.

To President HH, you must win this next election – if you don't, you will be responsible for the misery that Zambians will face post-election. Your party has the necessary structures and peoples to win a substantive election. All you need is a strategy (remember "Don't Kubeba" for the PF), you can defeat PF at their own game of rigging and corruption. If you fail to win, you will force people like me to leave my comfortable life in Canada and return to Zambia and lead a movement towards zero poverty, zero corruption and zero "undemocracies."

2 HH IS THE RIGHT MAN FOR THE JOB

[Published: December 3rd, 2014, *Zambia Watchdog*]

Since independence from British rule on October 24th, 1964, Zambia has been ruled by five[16] presidents: Kenneth Kaunda (KK); Frederick Chiluba; Levy Mwanawasa; Rupiah Banda; and Michael Sata. Contrary to popular but erroneous public opinion, only two of these presidents can be said to be a true or adjuvant to the Bemba tribe (Michael Sata and Frederick Chiluba). KK's parents could have hailed from Malawi, and there are no Bembas in Malawi. Mwanawasa was a member of the Lenje tribe and Banda is from the Nyanja.

In historical as well as political parlance, no tribe has dominated politics in Zambia as is often asserted.

---

[16] At the time this article was written, President Lungu had not been elected yet.

Kaunda was from Chinsali, but that does not make him a Bemba. In fact, a critical look at Zambian presidential history will show that the so-called Bemba presidents have proved to be more tribalistic than non-Bemba ones. Other than KK, no other president after him had a clear Tribal Balancing agenda. Although the late Sata accused both Mwanawasa and Banda of being tribalistic, he, Sata, happened to be the most tribal of all presidents.

If Zambians are honest with themselves, and if the interest of the nation is to supersede personal and political proclivities, of all the presidential contenders and potential contenders in the coming January 2015 presidential by-election, only one candidate stands out as credible – Hakainde Hichilema (HH). There are four reasons why Zambians should vote HH as the next president of Zambia.

First, the tribalism accusation against HH has no merit. HH has not been a leader of Zambia; he has not been elected as president before. He has never ruled Zambia, so why do some quarters still smear him with tribalism murk? Other than as a political gimmick to lure votes, there is no evidence whatsoever to suggest that HH is or will be tribalistic. HH is a Tonga, yes, but Tongas are not tribalistic. Zambia must be grateful to the likes of Mainza Chona who handed the first presidency of Zambia to the likes of KK freely. The Tongas – and more so their tribal cousins the Lozis – if they were stingy with power, could have been ruling Zambia since 1964. Their politicians were agile, educated and many times richer than others from other tribes. But, in the interest of harmony, they have, historically, chosen the path of peace and inclusiveness. A few of them here and there may be tribal in their politics, but that is to be expected in all other tribes as well. Michael Sata, a Bemba president, was even more tribalistic than all other presidents before him.

Second, HH, of all the candidates and potential candidates, comparatively, seems to have a more stable party, well-organized machine and less toxic personalities around him. One can also say that, comparatively, he has a better platform and agenda for Zambia than all other candidates.

Third, like Sata, HH has been a fighter. He has attempted to rule before but he either came in third or was rejected by the other tribes. But in all this, he has never withered; he has been consistent. This posture – which literally gave Sata the presidency – is alive and well in HH. HH will, more than any other candidate, help bring normalcy to Zambian politics and secure for Zambia a better economical legacy. And he is relatively young (we do not yet know who will emerge the PF candidate).

Fourth, and perhaps the most important, HH as president of Zambia is critical to accountability. If anyone of the aspiring candidates in PF becomes president, we may never know how the Sata regime abused power and squandered national coffers for personal gains. All the indignities and undemocratic tendencies perpetrated, especially during Sata's incapacity, may go unpunished. A win by the MMD could also ensure accountability, but it is doubtful whether that would be accomplished in good faith. There is just too much personal vendetta involved in the MMD aspirants (especially if Banda should be elected president). Besides, MMD is on record as a party of thieves and corrupters. The new leaders may be immune but the brand is tainted!

Zambia must give HH a chance to rule, especially if he

must be prodded to articulate his vision for Zambia in clear terms. It is best for Zambia in the interim. The PF win again is detrimental to the nation's wellbeing, especially to the democratic and developmental quests. None of the more than seven presidential candidates in the PF has a vision for Zambia. Sympathy for the dead is only welcome if a credible, formidable and believable leader was available in the PF. At the moment, there is none.

Zambia – push the assertion of tribalism aside, review history and analyze contemporary political events, and you find that Tongas and Lozis are not, and have never been, tribalistic. Some Bemba and Nyanja politicians portray them so. HH may make a sound president for Zambia – particularly at this crucial moment!

3 THE WAR ZAMBIA MUST FIGHT AND WIN

[Published: September 8th, 2012, *Lusaka Times*]

Rafeeah Mulla, a Grade Nine pupil at International School of Lusaka, in a *Zambia Daily Mail* newspaper clip of Saturday, November 5th, 2011, titled, "Zambia, 50 Years from Now," laments:

> Zambia's current population is thirteen million.[17] I estimate that fifty years from now it may double to twenty-six million; putting enormous strain on our meager resources, such as food, clothing, hospitals, infrastructure and so on. To keep up with our increasing population, Zambia needs to have a much larger economic growth rate than it has had in the last fifty years, especially if it wants to enjoy a better living standard in 2061 which I know we can achieve if we are really determined.

---

[17] In 2021, Zambia's population stood at 17.8 million

The astute student goes on and prescribes the parameters necessary to enable Zambia to emerge as a strong nation in terms of its economy and democracy: "For us to advance, we need a safe and peaceful country." Mulla then praises the efforts the country has made in developing democratic institutions and cultural edifices which collectively will and has continued to define Zambia as a free and accommodating nation.

On September 25th, 2011, UN Secretary-General[18] Ban Ki Moon hailed Zambia for setting "an example for the rest of Africa and the wider world about how power can be transferred peacefully." In fact, Zambia has been transferring power smoothly and peacefully since its creation in 1964. The UN Chief was on record for having chided other African nations to emulate Zambia in allowing democracy to flourish.

Despite Zambia being placed as one of the favorable recipients of donor aid in poverty reduction programs, there was nothing tangible to show for it in terms of bettering the lives of the majority poor

However, as it is often mused, democracy has been a feature of the African social mosaic even in pre-colonial days. The yardstick for measuring democracy in Africa has always been the Westernized concept of freedom and democratization, which have often been the holding of "free and fair" elections and the nudge for freedoms and other fundamental human rights to be deeply entrenched into the political fabric of the nation. That, truly, is commendable and even attractive at best. But what has been overlooked is the fact that democracy or good governance has not been African predominant problems.

---

[18] On January 1st, 2017, António Guterres took over from Ban Ki Moon as the ninth Secretary-General of the United Nations.

Social and economic indicators in so-called war-torn African states and the peaceful nations are not any different. It will be imprudent to farce that Nigeria, for example, which has had a good share of coups since its independence, lags Zambia in terms of economic development. The 54 states of Africa all have had one aspect of political or military struggle or the other. They all are, to a larger extent, products of a colonial past, a past imbued with tribal disruptions and political insipidity. That said, it cannot be construed as a blame-balm for Africa's future problems.

The past, notwithstanding, Africa's biggest problem is poverty, and this has nothing to do with what happened in the colonial or post-colonial eras. Those eras, of course, contributed, but cannot be used as an ante for harangue. In fact, unfortunate events like Colonialism should now equip Africa to deal with future problems effectively. Credit must be given to African leaders for trying to run their governments under very difficult circumstances, but more can and must be done. There can never be any excuse for poverty – it dehumanizes the soul and pulverizes a people's best intentions.

The MMD government in Zambia, in the run-up to the September 20th, 2011, elections recognized poverty as "Zambia's biggest problem." Dr. Guy Scott, then Vice-president of the Republic of Zambia, was on record as having said that, "Ordinary Zambians had been left out of the current growth in the country." In Zambia, despite the enormous economic spurts boosted by increased copper production, the conditions of the common person have not changed.

Poverty is inimical to a people's future well-being; it is a nation's enemy number one, and as such it must be combatted and defeated at all costs. Corruption, abuse of resources and neglect of industries which have been cited as causes of poverty in Zambia, are, in fact, the symptoms of poverty, and not the causes of it.

This is a norm, so it seems, regardless of which government is in power. Of course, there are those who think, erroneously, that under Kenneth Kaunda Zambia performed very well in economic terms. But this is only a case of short-sightedness, as Kaunda himself was defeated in the elections in 1991 because the people, and the International Financial Institutions, then, observed that the only remedy to the precarious Zambian economic facia was the Structural Adjustment Programs (SAPs). SAPs had become *anathema*, a case of throwing the baby with the water.

In the wake of the Euro Crisis in 2011-2012, such theorizing had been taken by events. SAPs regime is no longer seen as a panacea to Africa's, and indeed Europe's, decaying economic conditions. The two late Zambian presidents, Frederick Chiluba and Levy Mwanawasa, introduced economic liberalism in Zambia. Under this economic framework, the socialistic regime of Kaunda was replaced by one of free-market competition. Those who depended on hand-outs became the real victims of the new economic structure. Kaunda was no longer there to dish out cooking oil, mealie meal and so on.

Under the Rupiah Banda's regime, people still recognized poverty as the biggest problem. Civil Society for Poverty Reduction (CSPR) challenged former president Banda to make poverty a priority in the *Post* of Thursday, March 31st, 2011. And Marylyn Celli, a governance advocate, was bemused that despite Zambia being placed as one of the favorable recipients of donor aid in poverty reduction programs, there was nothing tangible to show for it in terms of bettering the lives of the majority poor.

Indeed, each year, Zambia and many other African countries, receive aid from donor governments and the co-operating partners. But poverty, for which majority of these funds is acquired, never seem to rescind; the people are not better than before aid was acquired.

The University of Zambia (UNZA) student body has been challenging governments to explain their plans for ending poverty in Zambia. Kelvin Chitala, one of the UNZA Student Union leaders once said that, "Zambians were in need of a government that would champion poverty eradication countrywide." This, unfortunately, has been a song for many years since Zambia attained to its political independence.

Zambia has a problem of poverty. According to Marcos Rodrigues, Cuban Foreign Deputy Minister, "Africa has enough talent to solve the continent's problems." And what President Michael Sata calls the "fruits of independence" can only be prosperity, which has eluded the Zambian people for over 40 years. Indeed, like former Bank of Zambia Governor, Caleb Fundanga, said, "Disparities between the rich and the poor will exist," however, this should not deter the Zambian governments from fighting this scourge.

Of course, corruption is a sister problem to poverty, but poverty supersedes corruption. In many cases, it is poverty which breeds corruption. Curbing poverty is the first step towards eradicating corruption.

African institutions have not been strengthened enough to attain to a system of imbedded checks and balances, like the West have. And the war that must be fought and won should be poverty, even before fighting other national scourges.

> POVERTY IS INIMICAL TO A PEOPLE'S FUTURE
> WELL-BEING; IT IS A NATION'S ENEMY
> NUMBER ONE, AND AS SUCH IT MUST BE
> COMBATTED AND DEFEATED AT ALL COSTS.
> CORRUPTION, ABUSE OF RESOURCES AND
> NEGLECT OF INDUSTRIES WHICH HAVE BEEN
> CITED AS CAUSES OF POVERTY IN ZAMBIA,
> ARE, IN FACT, THE SYMPTOMS OF POVERTY,
> AND NOT THE CAUSES OF IT.

The cancer that is eating up Zambia is poverty. It must be fought with all the might that government possesses. President Michael Sata and his government must ensure that their fight is the fight against poverty. The dignity of the people of Zambia depends on it. The future of Zambia relies on it. And the sanity of a people is in pursuance to it. Poverty is Zambia's enemy number one, and it must be conquered at all cost!

4 A THOUSAND THOUGHTS FOR ZAMBIA

[10th Anniversary ZAMCAN Speech, 2010]

I have a thought welling in my heart concerning our nation [Zambia]. I will borrow from the Canadian journalist Pierre Berton who stated: "A poor man is not free and a destitute man is as much a prisoner as a convict; indeed a convict generally eats better. A man who can't afford a streetcar ticket, let alone real travel, who can exercise no real choice in matters of food, clothing, and shelter, who cannot follow the siren song of the commercial, who can scarcely afford bus fair to the library let alone a proper education for himself or his children – is such a man free...?"

As I read those lines my mind raced, my heart pounded and my strength whined. For then I began to realize that such is the state of affairs of many people back home in Zambia. A situation such as this one makes me wonder whether we are truly free as a nation. If freedom means being poor and miserable, then I would rather be in prison, Berton seems to be suggesting. And yet the reality at home is exactly as he has described.

Do we hold some keys to the development of Zambia as the "privileged" ones in the diaspora? We definitely know the difference between responsible living and oblivion; clean water and no water at all; combed surroundings and homelessness; discarding left-overs and going without food for three or more days. In that sense alone, living and working in Canada is a privilege. But as the saying goes, "Home is Home," we are bound, as it were, to remember that we have a home, and Zambia is that home.

Let us not forget, we are not free until we can champion our own destiny. And we are not free here either when the majority of our friends, relatives, acquaintances, and our own fresh and blood are not free back there. Africa in general and Zambia in particular, continues to wallow in poverty. And that is not freedom. Our governments are doing their best, the international community is doing what it can, and the multilaterals are trying their magic. But Zambia can only be redeemed by its own people - we the people of Zambia. There are many ways in which we can help build our nation. And one way is sure, especially for us in the diaspora.

The answer to the question I asked earlier - do we hold some keys to the development of Zambia? - is yes, we do. And I believe it starts by valuing what we have. Zamcan[19] is ours to build. Zamcan is Zambia in miniature. It is ours to nurture, keep and perfect. When we build Zamcan collectively, we are also building Zambia indirectly. We can enshrine a mentality of brotherhood, nationalism, and patriotism as we labor together to perfect Zamcan. From here we can defuse a character of progressive Zambianism that may reach to the banks of the River Zambezi and water our mortified legacies.

In the diaspora, we can influence decisions back home and offer informed solutions to many of the problems facing our leaders. We cannot wait to be involved; we should take it upon ourselves. The experiences and expertise we have accumulated can be the very seeds needed to transform our economy and society into a land of personal freedom, limited governance, consent of the governed, reformed liberalism, and decency for the many poor among the population.

---

[19] See footnote #5

5 ZAMBIA IS NOT A PROVINCE IN NIGERIA

[Written between 2006 and 2010]

"Do you guys have fridges, stoves, electricity?" This was not the first time I had heard such sentiments about Africa. My wife tells me about an experience she had the first time she went to university in Canada. A professor asked her whether she knew how to start a computer, meaning... can an African really do a good job? Whilst in St. Catharines, I was repeatedly asked about Zambia, and to my surprise, very few people know about Zambia. Some even thought that Zambia was one of the provinces of Nigeria.

No, Zambia is not a province of any country in Africa. Zambia is a sovereign nation with its own government. Like the map on your left shows, Zambia is sandwiched in the middle of eight other countries in Central-southern Africa. And Zambia is not in a dark bushy jungle. There is electricity in most urban towns and people use computers and all that technology promises. In fact, in Lusaka alone, there are so many cars that it is hardly possible to cross the Cairo Road.

Albeit, Zambia is a developing country, meaning she's not there quite yet at the level of USA or Canada. But that does not mean that people don't reasonably enjoy life and freedom. There is so much to appreciate here – the culture, the people, natural surroundings, tourism attractions, and many more. Some parts of Zambia are so developed that you would think you were in the middle of Scarborough. The only problem seems to be the unsustainable nature or the inconsistencies in planning.

Poverty issue in Zambia? Yes, but not at the expense of the raging disparity. In economic terms, this is translated a poor nation. But let us face it; 20 percent% of the people enjoy 80 percent of the nation's wealth. That's why the country is poor, not that it does not have economic resources. Eighty-six percent of the people live below the poverty line – that is a big challenge. That means that there is a handful who amass what the majority should be sharing.

6 ZAMBIA – COMPARED TO ONTARIO & SWITZERLAND

[Published: March 11th, 2019, *Lusaka Times, Muckrack*]

Here is my thinking and a challenge to all Zambians. We have a very tiny economy and we spend a great deal of our time fighting over a pint of salt when we could be mining the ocean. I reside in Ontario, Canada's largest province. Ontario is only a province in Canada – but it's by far richer than Zambia, a nation-state. Consider, for example, Ontario has a population of about 15 million people. But it boasts of a GDP of over US$660 billion. Ontario's main industries include Manufacturing, Hydro (electricity), Film & Media, Tech, Telecommunications, Steel, Agriculture. The average annual income for Ontario is about US$45,000.[20]

Ontario compares favorably, even at par with Switzerland, which has a population of about nine million people. Switzerland's GDP is over US$685 billion. Switzerland's main industries include Pharma, Finance and Tennis. And, on average, an individual earns about US$61,000 per year in Switzerland.

Zambia, on the other hand, has a population of about 16 million people,[21] statistically the same as Ontario's. But Zambia's GDP is very small, at about US$26 billion. Zambia's major industries include copper mining and processing, construction, emerald mining, beverages, food, textiles, chemicals, fertilizer and horticulture. The

---

[20] As of March 2019
[21] In 2019

highest paid Zambian may earn about US$66,000 per year.

What does these numbers say? First, that Zambia is under-utilizing its resources (human, raw, capital, and so on) and underdeveloping its potential. But it remains, relatively, a very small economy, more like a province of some small country in Europe. Second, there is need to change the focus. Focus, has generally, been on arguing about the small resources in circulation (mostly centred around copper mining) rather than growing the pie. There is urgent need to increase GDP, expand industries, and make copper mining subsidiary to agriculture, for example. And third and last, compared to Switzerland (which has tennis and finance at the core of its economy and yet is far richer than Zambia), Zambia has potential to develop its existing industries, invest in and develop new others, and become a prosperous country.

Zambia can become a higher-income earner. This is not simply intellectual pandering; there are steps that can be taken to achieve an Upper-Income Economic status. I have proposed a 30-10-60 Theory[22] in earlier writings.

The gist of the 30-10-60 economic model is that, within the next 50 years, Zambia should attain to an affluent middle-class characterized by, "being able to enjoy an acceptable standard of living and being happy (happiness will mean having a life expectancy of 76 years and above; enjoying and having access to a stable and working social support system; freedom from corruption; being able to give to others; and ability to bring in an income that meets all the basic needs and have surplus for saving for the future)."

---

[22] See Chapter 7

7 THE 30-60-10 UPPER-INCOME ECONOMIC THEORY

[Published: January 18th, 2019, *charlesmwewa.com*]

In the next 50 years, Africa will be the new global economic leader. This will be, notably, the most sustainable economic paradigm shift the world has ever witnessed. This is not mere presumption or a dream, global indicators are in every place. For the start, the rise of Africa is poised to be a natural mutation for three reasons. First, the West and other transitory rich nations will have plateaued (technically, reached their highest summits) and will have no room for going any further but slowing down. Second, the faultiness in Western formations in terms of economic and political framing are growing more and more uncertain with each passing year. And third, social and ideological polarity in presently model democracies are but a sign of future trouble.

But juxtapose the above scenario with Africa. The past of Africa is its bridge to the future. And Africa's past means only one thing: Resilience. Africa has endured slave trade and Colonialism – and has emerged forgiving, determined to re-write history and is focused on re-defining its future impact. Africans have been vilified as a race of people, de-nationalized as national states, censured as rational, intelligent beings, and overtly ruled out of technological competition. And yet, in defiant of, and against all odds, African nations remain relatively united, open, welcoming and integrated. The anomaly has been that, in discussions dealing with Africa, Africa is "globalized" and not individualized. For example, Africa has 54 countries, and only 15 of these are in some sort of conflict: "There are currently fifteen African countries involved in war, or are experiencing post-war conflict and tension."[23] This represents about 28%, and not 100% as international reports seem to suggest. According to the Institute for Economics and Peace, only Botswana, Chile, Costa Rica, Japan, Mauritius, Panama, Qatar, Switzerland, Uruguay and Vietnam can be considered truly free from conflict. In short, while more and more countries in America, Europe and Asia are tending towards conflict, Africa is more and more trending towards peace and unity. In economic parlance, peace and solidarity are catalysts for prosperity and economic investment. Africa will have both by 2070.

The most interesting of African economic story will be told from Zambia. In terms of national character, Zambia has four factors that will catapult her to uncommon prosperity and economic growth. These are: The people are peaceful; the people are diligent and industrious; the people love knowledge and experimenting; and Zambians tend to be democratic in approaches to governance. Anyone who may argue against these four, either is peremptorily biased or has not studied Zambia the way I have done.

The above, notwithstanding, the necessary impetus for Zambian change is to have a mixture of true economic growth and prosperity while enhancing the happiness of the people based on what I call a "30-60-10 Upper-Income Economic Theory." From a policy perspective, "30-60-10" means 30% of population is upper-class; 60% middle-class; and 10% lower-class. In this paradigm,

---

[23] *Africa Sun News* – "Africa Wars and Conflicts"

middle-class will be defined as being able to enjoy an acceptable standard of living and being happy (happiness will mean having a life expectancy of 76 years and above; enjoying and having access to a stable and working social support system; freedom from corruption; being able to give to others; and ability to bring in an income that meets all the basic needs and to have surplus for saving for the future). In short, the middle-class is an affluent class. The upper-class will be those who exceed the middle-class definition, and the lower-class are those who fall short of the middle-class definition.

The future of Zambia lies in the deliberate restoration and empowerment of the middle-class. In this Zambia, the middle-class will not be the engine of the economy; they will be the heart and soul of the economy. This economy will be designed to grow from bottom-up. Rebuilding the middle-class and maintaining it at around 60% is key. The rich or upper-class do not grow the economy unless they can create jobs. A large percentage of the lower-class means less productivity and more dependence on government handout. The goal will be to move a large chunk of the poor population into the middle-class (by deliberate government's action that legislatively creates an enabling environment for fair competition).

The result of this economic paradigm is to reverse the historical inequalities created by the imposition of structural adjustments that work for Western cultures but totally fail in Africa. And they have failed because (1) African ideology is neither Socialism nor Capitalism; it's a combination of many factors, including welfare Capitalism and a form of Socialism that minimizes social proprietorship and maximizes a democratic control of the means of production. This balance is essential to reducing the gaping social and economic inequalities among the population; (2) African leadership and democracy must be redefined; and (3) African innovative spirit, free experimentation has been mischaracterized.

In future articles, I will elaborate on (2) and (3) above and will provide parameters for formulating policy as well as the embalming of a diligent and corrupt-free culture that ensures the paradigm's success and survival.

8 UNJUSTIFIED POVERTY IN ZAMBIA

[Published: November 9th, 2012, *The African Executive*]

Poverty in Zambia is unwarranted, and even unexplained. Zambia subscribes to two economic conundrums: The fact that all the factors that make nations wealthy are present; and the fact that all the conditions that make nations poor are fairly non-existent. In spite of that, the nation is still poor and struggling.

Good Institutions but Still Poor

The brightest of economics' minds in the world have failed to explain why the major factors attributive in *Why Nations Fail* by Acemoglu and Robinson are not applicable to Zambia, and yet the nation is still one of the poorest in the world. Zambia has good political and democratic institutions, conducts free and fair elections every five years, is rich in mineral and climatic wealth, and has relatively credible infrastructures that exploit its resources. Most economic commentators identify good laws and practices that motivate people to work hard as conveyor-belts for economic productivity. These, they assert, help to enrich both citizens and nations alike. Zambia is rich in both.

Zambia's relatively history of good government has permitted good institutions to take shape. This is despite the nation being only about 48 years old. A sincere disservice that most economic theories postulate is that, for Africa in general, and for countries like Zambia in particular, the people have not had enough time to absorb or otherwise unlearn their long history of tribal organization. In short, tribal organization is construed as a recipe for poverty in years to come. The assumption is that long lines of tribal chiefs have not empowered their subjects towards independent rational thinking as well as towards true economic freedom. Those who advance this thesis actually argue strongly, ironically, that Britain, for example, has benefited from its monarchial establishment, while those from chiefdom-type establishments have not.

This posture does not explain why Zambia is poor, either. In fact, the pre-colonial Zambian regimes worked to encourage tribal governance rather to decimate it.

Through Indirect Rule, African chiefs were given mandates, albeit salaciously, to continue to rule the locals on pre-imperial patterns. By October 1964, Zambia was already being governed from Lusaka, evidence that a strong central government was deeply entrenched into the Zambian political proclivity.

Reversal of Fortunes

Africa has experienced what is termed as "the reversal of fortune." This is mostly attributed to European Imperialism, especially at the end of the 19th Century. At some time in the past Peru, Indonesia, and India were very wealthy nations; the African continent as well was. European imperialists, however, introduced corrupt "extractive" economic institutions, such as forced labor and confiscation of produce, to drain wealth and labor from the natives. In other words, the governing elites extracted incomes and wealth from the masses in order to enrich themselves. As uncouth and unpalatable politically as this postulation may seem, it still does not explain why a country like Zambia is poor.

A quick visit to one of the Zambian shanty compounds will reveal that people there live in conditions too despicable for human habitation. They sleep in conditions too drastic to be described. They eat once per day and carry on their day-to-day affairs in situations too inglorious to be explained. Yet, even the most human of the Zambian politicians just resign themselves to mere maintainers of the *status quo* when they get in power. The national infrastructure is in deplorable conditions. Some bridges are as old as Zambia itself; some prisons as small as when the population of the country was only 3.5 million and still catering for a population of 13 million. Hospital spaces, medical equipment and medicines, are in critical supply. Schools, and even the University of Zambia, are in unspeakable conditions – students and pupils alike barely survive, jeopardising both the quality and delivery of education. The Lusaka (Kenneth Kaunda) International Airport, still the same capacity as when it was built over 30 years ago, remains the same size and in deplorable conditions. City centers and towns are harbingers of disease and dirt; roads are in serious state of disrepair, with lethal potholes; and people die just when they reach their most productive ages. Once in a while a new building or sets of buildings or malls or hotels pop out in some place, and there is great jubilation and celebration. And yet, such so-called developments have been long overdue – by the time certain ills and conditions of society are addressed, people have contracted diseases and even passed on. There is no sense of urgency on the part of the rulers; and there is no sense of spirit for protest on the part of the ruled. It's as if the governors and the governed have come to accept their conditions as fate. And worse still, credible institutions of the Bretton Woods keep satiating the economic image of Zambia with pontificated appraisals, such as the recent statement issued by the IMF mission that, "Zambia's economy prospects of 2013 look good with real Gross Domestic Product (GDP) growth expected to be at eight percent while inflation is expected to be at six percent." Who is benefiting?

Election debates are fuelled by politics of personality while issues that affect the majority are bypassed. Major media outlets like the electronic and print either report on what excite them and otherwise promote their philosophy and whims or are politically news based.

There is generally a parochial worship of foreign-driven development, which for the most part, is only a conduit of neo-colonial punditry. A sense of the now blurs the efforts to invest for the future. An acceptance of politically-defined progress limits the nation's capacity to stretch itself further and explore new ideas, new ventures and new ways of approaching development.

The Curse of Mineral Resources

Citations and including those nominated by the C.I.A all seem to highlight the mineral resources of Zambia more as a curse than a blessing. The so-called "curse of natural resources" has been depicted in statements like, "Zambia's economy has experienced strong growth in recent years, with real GDP growth in 2005-11 of more than six percent per year. Privatization of government-owned copper mines in the 1990s relieved the government from covering mammoth losses generated by the industry and greatly increased copper mining output and profitability to spur economic growth. Copper output has increased steadily since 2004, due to higher copper prices and foreign investment." Just when you think this salutation is sustainable, and then you read, "Poverty remains a significant problem in Zambia, despite a stronger economy."

A conundrum so devastating to national ethos, a statement so damaging to national conscious; an appraisal so demeaning to the national intellect; and an elegy to the nation's productive future – this salutation remains a Zambian curse. Moreover, and to add insult to injury, between 2005 and 2006, Zambia qualified for debt relief under the Highly Indebted Poor Country Initiative.

About US$6 billion was forgiven in debt relief. One would have thought that the politicians' foremost excuse for poverty in the country was dealt with, alas; poverty has remained a significant problem in Zambia. And other excuses have been advanced.

If Zambia's dependency on copper makes it vulnerable to depressed commodity prices as has been postulated, the period between 2005 and 2012 has refuted that claim. For in that period, the nation has recorded high copper prices in addition to a bumper maize crop between 2010 and 2012. Moreover, Zambia, in economic terms, was barely affected by the 2008 world economic crunch. Yet, countries that were affected by the credit melt-down of 2008 have recovered and are still richer; Zambia still remains poor and one of the poorest in the world.

The HIV/AIDS Excuse

Zambia had a high birth rate, of approximately 43.51 births/1,000 population in 2012. Zambia's death rate stands at 12.42 deaths/1,000 population in July 2012. The implications are huge. It is this dynamic that is material to the poverty debate rather than the HIV/AIDS excuse. While on one hand, there has been emphasis on fighting the HIV/AIDS pandemic, which some see as a menace to the productive age of the Zambian demographic, there has been, on the other, a denial that considering the number of births apropos to deaths in Zambia, the biggest problem, as far as poverty is concerned, has been in controlling the population spurts. The reason often advanced is that a relatively high HIV/AIDS burden and market distorting agricultural policies have meant that Zambia's economic growth has not dramatically decreased the stubbornly high poverty rates. This, too, does not explain why there is poverty in Zambia.

No Political Instability but Still Poor

By purchasing power party (PPP), the ten poorest countries in Africa, namely Congo DR ($400), Liberia ($500), Zimbabwe ($500), Burundi ($600), Somalia ($600), Eritrea ($700), Central African Republic ($800), Niger ($800), and with the exception of Madagascar ($900), and Malawi ($900), have all been dogged by civil wars or critical political conditions. Zambia has not. On the contrary, Zambia boasts of inclusive economic and political institutions that distribute power broadly in society and which are subject to constraints. In Zambia, power is not vested in a single individual or a narrow group; there is a thriving caucus of opposition political parties, and a truly remarkable and well-groomed civil society. And yet, and despite all the liberal democratic pluses, Zambia is still poor.

Disease Does Not Cause Poverty

Diseases cannot be blamed for poverty, because even as Acemoglu and Robinson have argued, "Disease is largely a consequence of poverty and of governments being unable or unwilling to undertake the public health measures necessary to eradicate them." Although tropical diseases like malaria kill a lot of children in Zambia, UNICEF has vouched that malaria has been under control, for "Zambia has made strides in malaria prevention and control in the last five years." The numbers of deaths arising from malaria in Zambia per year is 8000. This is not worse in comparison to Canada where about 75,700 people will die from cancer alone in 2012. Similarly, some analysts' arguments that, "Europe has glaciated fertile soils, reliable summer rainfall, and few tropical diseases; tropical Africa has unglaciated and extensively infertile soils, less reliable rainfall, and many tropical diseases," only partly explains why certain countries like Zambia are still poor. Agricultural productivity has little to do with soil quality. The case of the Nile Delta is germane to this debate. It has nothing to do with the "ownership structure of the land and the incentives that are created for farmers by the governments and institutions under which they live," either. Zambia has one of the most liberal policies in the world in as far as land is concerned. And Zambians are among the most hard-working peoples on the global.

Zambian Culture Does Not Promote Poverty

Some blame a work culture in Zambia. Critical analysis does not support that premise, either. The Zambian work situation will reveal that it is more of the work policies and not a work culture. Zambian work culture and philosophies generally support hard work, industry and diligence. A microscopic evaluation of the Zambian village lends credence to this assertion. There, people till their land from morning till evening. There, people have traditionally been self-sufficient for centuries. There, laziness is not only undesirable, but is spurned upon as a societal ill.

Real Action is Required

What is germane to the poverty debate is that a conscientious government addresses the problem without giving undue excuses. Addressing questions of why Zambia is poor have been the preoccupation of social scientists for the past forty years, and no tangible results have been achieved for the majority poor Zambians so far. Co-relating the presence or prevalence of war or famine in some countries; the role of effective central governments; the deleterious effect of corruption and corrupt government officials; and the over-used platitude of "resource-rich but lack capital needed to create infrastructures," mantras are all only bywords.

What is required is *this* government, in concert with the *people* themselves, to frown upon poverty, treat it like a deadly disease, for so it is, and move heaven and earth to remove it, permanently. What is required is doing; not talking. What is required is creating many opportunities; not proposing alternatives. What is required is using the profit from copper sells to create jobs for the unemployed, improve dilapidated schools and hospitals, resuscitate national infrastructure and erase shanty-compounds and create modern housing in their place. What is required is an ambitious program to rid the town-centers of squalors, street vendors and in their place create clean and responsible and taxable ventures. What is required is a policy on sanitation that penalizes anyone vandalising public property or throwing garbage[24] elsewhere other than in designated bins or urinating in open places rather than in well-maintained public

---

[24] Rubbish

washrooms,[25] and etc. What is required under President Michael Sata is: ignore conventionalism of educate and empower the people and who will in turn change their situations. That has not worked for over 40 years. Simply do it; create and act and end poverty.

---

[25] Toilets

9 DOMICILITY CLAUSE

[Published: November 18th, 2019, *Lusaka Times, Muckrack*]

There are several motivations the drafters of the current *Constitution* had in mind when they placed the Domicility Clause (DC) in our current highest law in the country. One of those motivations is pure foolishness. I wake up on the shores of Lake Ontario and admire the azure morning dews on the meadows and I sigh, "What a brilliant country, a brilliant world we live in." I have never doubted that Canada, for example, is an epitome of what and how a country and people should live. It is a model in almost every dimension – human rights, industry, technology, prosperity, academia and the list is endless. I live here and work here and have contributed my energy, intellect and I also lecture in its prestigious institutions – day-after-day contributing to the expansive knowledge base that make Canada a world's beacon.

And here comes a Zambian politician who says, "No, he can't come and vie for presidency here because he has not been in Zambia for 10 or so years!" Thinking this is patriotism – what retrogressive thinking. But before you indict me with insults and insipid mindlessness, let me tell you what you want to say. "You see, you want to double-dip – you want to have the best of the two worlds – you want to have a decent life abroad and then come and take away our positions!" If this is not foolishness, then it is the lowest form of ignorance. Because it will not be loss but an addition for me to return and contribute, for all purposes and intentions.

You don't know the history of independent Africa. Africa was liberated by people who lived abroad and these influenced greatly the locals. They learned all the wisdom and secrets and even the hidden agendas of their Western counterparts and from then resolved to liberate Africa. They had to, first, understand the psychology of politics and the mindset that had enslaved or colonized them. They then knew how to "fight" for independence and self-determination. Africa would not have been liberated apart from those who got educated and who worked abroad. To develop Africa, the same trend must continue.

There are two advantages that those of us who have lived and worked in developed formations have over those of you who have spent all your life in Africa. First, we live and work with our American and European counterparts and we understand them better. When we run African governments, we will be least duped and "cheated" because we understand the concepts and ideals that set these countries apart from the rest. And second and last, we have tested the "engine" of the West and, therefore, we can relate to ideas like technology, monetary policies, democratic indices and human right indicators. If it comes to negotiating for viable economic policies and agendas, no-one who has not lived in these countries can outwit us.

The truth is, you can give a Zambian who has never lived in a developed country a job of a president and liberally permit him to rule for ten or more years, but the more years he rules, the worst the country will turn out. Give me the reigns and within two years I will develop the country. The reason is simple, I have lived in these developed formations for many years and I will, naturally, be more inclined to improving rather than degrading the brand.

Furthermore, our world is now a global village, and the implications are such that technology and knowledge are no longer a monopoly of one country. And the best people to transmit such knowledge and know-how will, naturally, be those who have lived and experienced Westernism firsthand. I submit that the fears those selfish and poorly-informed politicians had of imputing the DC into our Constitution had are not founded.

We are not here in the developed terrains for ourselves. We love our native countries and we would like to be back and contribute at the highest level. Change the Constitution and remove the DC from the highest national instrument. It is not only bullish; it is an impotent clause and can hinder the very progress that the nation desires and admires. Take way the DC and let those Zambians who have lived abroad come back and inject their experiences, knowledge, expertise, know-how and transferred-skills into development for all.

10 TEN REASONS WHY DUAL CITIZENSHIP IS GOOD FOR ZAMBIA

[Published: July 2nd, 2015, *Pambazuka*]

Most people oppose dual citizenship because they think that people in the diaspora already enjoy life there. As such, the addition of dual citizenship is seen as a bloated advantage. This is not correct.

This article is a response to Eric Chanda, president of Fourth Revolution Party (4R), who is ardent at opposing the inclusion of dual citizenship into the Zambian Constitution. On June 16th, 2015, Chanda opined that such an inclusion would only serve to "benefit foreigners." He called on Zambians outside to return to Zambia and help develop the country. He feared failure to doing so was tantamount to "hiding in the diaspora." Of course, the 4R leader played the issue of dual citizenship down in relation to other more nuanced economic-impact factors.

The factors most oft-quoted include the holding of a second passport; ability to find refuge in a safer country of dual citizenship if there is civil war or war in the resident country; for non-US citizens, ability to pay taxes only to one nation; ease of mobility, including an expansive array of investment opportunities in the two countries; freedom from economic mismanagement of one of the countries; and others.

Some argue against dual citizenship as a way of denying those in the diaspora another avenue of continuous acquisition of the better things of life. There is another reason: Former vice-president, Enoch Kavindele, once saw the granting of dual citizenship as a security risk, especially if one with dual citizenship was to rule as president.

One would not immediately fail to see that petty jealousies are usually at play. Sentiments like, "They are already better, what more do they want back home?" are frequently heard. And sometimes, there is a justifiable reasoning for saying so. The author remembers before he left for the diaspora hearing of stories of the diaspora and that living there automatically made one rich and "developed." And, for most people, this belief is highly preferred. In novels by Nigerian authors the term "been-to" became popularized in the 1980s and which caused many African students to desire to relocate as a means of enhancing their economic status. These stories, beliefs and sometimes misinformation, have collectively made some people to make leaving Africa and situating in rich and developed countries as their life-time and must-achieve goals. The reality is it is not always so, usually.

It is not the purpose of this article to present reasons for why sometimes relocating abroad is not a better dream than staying at home. That will be for another time. However, it is sufficient to mention that times have changed and the diaspora does not guarantee riches and a better life any more than education does not automatically guarantee one the best jobs available (but we all agree that education is a necessary condition for employment). Hard working, resourcefulness, good personal management, sound economic policies at work, sacrifice and discipline and sometimes a sheer stroke of luck, are needed to succeed, both abroad and at home. In addition, globalization has made the world a small village, where one needs not travel abroad to benefit from development in any country on earth.

Indeed, dual citizenship has benefits for all. Just look at nations that allow it. These countries, in alphabetical orders, allow dual citizenship either completely or with some modifications: Albania; Australia; Barbados; Bangladesh; Belgium; Bulgaria; Canada; Chile; Costa Rica; Croatia; Cyprus; Czech Republic; Egypt; Finland; France; Germany; Greece; Hungary; Iceland; Israel; Italy; Jamaica; Kosovo; Latvia; Malta; Mexico; Pakistan; Panama; Peru; Philippines; Portugal; Romania; Serbia; Slovenia; South Africa; South Korea; Spain; Sweden; Switzerland; Syria; Turkey; United Kingdom; and the United States. It can be argued here that these countries, combined, control the largest share of global wealth and most promote citizens' liberties and democracy. These countries saw it economically viable to allow for dual citizenship.

There are also other countries which do not allow for dual citizenship, and even this is not in all instances, and these are: Andorra; Austria; China; Denmark; India (with modifications); Japan (completely disallows); Malaysia; Netherlands; Norway; Panama; Poland; Singapore; Thailand; Ukraine (with modifications); United Arab Emirates; and Venezuela.

Countries not listed in either list above either have no official policy or legislation on dual citizenship, or like Zambia, are in the process of legislating for the same. But Zambia's situation is peculiar and demands context. Addressing Zambians in South Africa recently, President Lungu said, "Government has agreed to allow Zambians to hold dual citizenship with some rights like the presidency (contesting presidential elections) being the preserve of those holding single citizenship."

I knew that there was a side of this president, which is smart, wise, reasonable and caring. And this side understands that dual citizenship in the case of Zambia is a national asset, not a mark of double-dipping. There is not so much to double-dip for in Zambia. In honesty, if most people living in the developed countries where asked to choose between Zambia and those countries, I have no doubt they would choose those countries. At the moment, those countries promise relative political stability, economic wellness, social freedom. They also provide better pay for relatively the same jobs in Zambia and have lower unemployment rates and very high life expectancy rates. Therefore, it cannot be a question of choice between Zambia and say, the USA; it is more than politics, economics or wanting a better life.

Most of us advocate for dual citizenship because of our love for Zambia, albeit poor, struggling and, plainly, with nothing globally to write home about. Patriotism drives us. The same reason why we write commentaries, participate in social media forums and contribute on law and development in Zambia. We love Zambia and want to see the nation progress from poverty to prosperity.

The inclusion of dual citizenship clause in the *Zambian Constitution* may be justified on ten grounds:

First, the "first African leaders" benefited from exposure abroad: Those who liberated Africa were mostly groomed in the West, and a few from China and Russia. Under Colonialism, a number of young African scholars were going abroad, typically to the "mother" country, to acquire good education. After independence from the colonial rulers, many Africans continued to go to Europe for education that would enable them to promote well-being in their home countries upon return.[26] It is debatable whether the education they acquired abroad was necessary to develop Africa, but it is incontestable that it helped them to liberate Africa.

Second, dual citizens can receive the benefits and privileges offered by each country. For example, they have access to two social service systems, can vote in either country or may be able to run for office in either country (depending on each country's laws). They are also allowed to work in either country without needing a work permit or VISA and can attend school in either country at the citizen tuition rate.[27] Why is this important to Third World formations like Zambia? Zambia is still grappling with an undeveloped education system. For the most part its teachers are inadequately trained, the facilities are either dilapidated or not there, and generally, educational standards are below the standards of those of the developed formations, like Canada or the USA. It is not being at variance to conclude that leaders trained from the developed educational background will have more to give in terms of leadership, value and ideas. They may also be able to live out what has worked abroad.

---

[26] Constant and Tien, 2010
[27] Jean Folger

Third, being trained abroad and living abroad are not the same things, therefore, only those who live abroad will have a sustained impact on the politics and economics of the poor formations. Take as an example a person who spends five years in college or university abroad. This person will perhaps be on a VISA or some sort of study permit and has limited access to resources and in most cases, will have limited mobility. When this person returns home, other than what they learned through "osmosis," they have nothing more than classroom experience of the developed formation. In short, though trained abroad, these "Western educated Africans" will still be African-minded in terms of policing and programming. It is not that African education is not adequate to develop Africa; it is a truism that most of what is in Africa is either imported from the developed countries or has their blessings. Talk of books, technology, leadership paradigms, even the sources of money used in Africa, these for the most part, come or have been borrowed from the rich countries. In recent past, Zambian presidents have gone and died abroad. It cannot be because Zambia has no medical facilities; it is because Zambians know, implicitly or explicitly, that better medical facilities are still found abroad.

Fourth, and as an addendum to three above, "Foreign-educated leaders attract more Foreign Direct Investment (FDI) to their country. Our rationale is that education obtained abroad encompasses a whole slew of factors that can make a difference in FDI flows when this foreign-educated individual becomes a leader."[28] FDI is a much needed currency in Zambia's quest to wean itself from the aura of central government. However, and even

---

[28] Constant and Tien, 2010

more importantly, foreign companies and governments may trust those who got their education and business experience from abroad and even more those who lived and worked abroad. If a president is one who lived and worked abroad, you can imagine the level of trust in his/her government. It is also important to emphasize that citizens who have lived abroad may, comparatively, be less corrupt, less dictatorial, less autocratic, less dishonest, and more democratic and fairer in their approach to governance. The reason is simple, because they lived and absorbed those values which most developed countries subscribe to.

Fifth, the idea of "Brain Earn" comes to light. Remember in the late 1980s and early 1990s when the concept of "brain drain" was rife on the political tongue. Now, the idea of brain drain is becoming obsolete and more so with increased global economic integration in place. Relocation or immigration does not drain brains anymore, it empowers brains. In other words, training or living in another country shapes your brain to infinite possibilities in terms of economic modelling, political idealization or social industry. A leader who has spent ten years squarely in Africa will be less industrious, less innovative, and less dexterous than another who lived or worked abroad, especially in the developed country. This is the same reason why developed governments may appoint leaders who have lived in Africa to head undertakings whose mission involve Africa.

Sixth, a dual citizen can own property in either country. This benefits both countries, but especially the poor country. The reason is simple, some countries restrict land ownership to citizens only and land or property is a genuine investment. Imagine more Zambians owning property, land and businesses abroad.

Imagine what this will do to promoting Zambian brands, connecting local businesses to the developed ones and generally putting Zambia on the map as has been the case for Israel, Nigeria or India. And this is not new, major corporations from the developed countries do own lands and properties and businesses in Africa. They can relocate interests based on the viability of the enterprise or enabling economic environment in either country. This benefit is self-assertive.

Seventh, dual citizenship informs cultural education. "Having dual citizenship gives you the chance to educate others about the culture and people of two different countries. Governments may like dual citizenship because it helps to promote a country's image and culture abroad. If you have two passports, you may have more access to the world."[29] Even more, it enhances tourism and promotes a healthy image abroad. Consider the Jews and the impact they have had in the USA, Canada, and UK. Consider the Nigerians, Jamaicans and to some extent, the Indians. All these nationals have made their birth countries powerful abroad. In international parlance, that means economic boom and political propagation of their originating countries.

Eighth, dual citizenship entails ease of travel. If you are a dual citizen, you enjoy the protection of two governments even when you are traveling. If you encounter problems on the trip, you can appeal to one or both governments' embassies. "When asked for identification during international travels, you can supply the passport that is least likely to raise eyebrows or cause problems among officials. You can also travel to both countries as a native citizen, avoiding the lengthy airport

---

[29] Kate Bradley

queues and questioning about your purposes."[30] This is self-explanatory.

Ninth, dual citizenship promotes increased security awareness. To a dual citizen, one country may be a homeland but the other is very much a new home. Immediately this will cause them to fully experience and embrace the ideals of both countries. Dual citizens will more likely than mono-citizens promote peace and order in both countries because of dual security interests in both. They will also be more sensitive to issues of war, terrorism and treason. This is the very opposite of the fears most people have of dual citizenship. Dual citizens, by design, are incapable of compromising the security secrets of both countries. They will likely defend both interests with equal strength. Their own safety depends on it.

Tenth, there is a trend towards world citizenship. One question that cannot be avoided now is: Where is the world going? The world is trekking towards more integration, globalization and outsourcing of important jobs and ideas. In light of this, duality of citizenship will not be too much to ask for. The only caveat under this clarion is that no-one nation should take advantage of another in economic and security terms. Done properly and lawfully, both countries stand to benefit from dual citizenship.

For Zambia, this is a move in the right direction. And for President Lungu, this is the best investment of his presidency to date. For the Zambian Parliamentarians currently voting on the adoption of the Constitution Bill, the issue of dual citizenship is not for the benefit of this author (because he will doubly benefit), it is for the

---

[30] Kate Bradley

benefit of the country. It is not Canada or the USA which stands to benefit, it is Zambia. Zambia will not make economic, political or social progress unless one of its sons or daughters who has been educated, worked and lived abroad (especially in a developed country) is allowed to become head of state.

11 WILL ZAMBIA BECOME A MATURE DEMOCRACY?

[Published: January 8th, 2015, *Pambazuka*]

Is 2015 the year of change in Zambia? With the 20 January presidential by-election fast approaching, will there be a shift from a growing democracy to a mature democracy? Can the nation finally shed the coat of corruption and become a truly democratic society that can trust and rely on its elected officials?

"And pity, like a naked newborn babe, striding the blast, or heaven's cherubim, horsed upon the sightless couriers of the air, shall blow the horrid deed in every eye, that tears shall drown the wind," Shakespeare's Macbeth depicting a seemly innocent deed with horrible connotations. That has been the story of Zambia for the past fifty years – the start has always been promising; the end horrible, especially for the majority poor. The same has been true in the choice of leadership. Whenever a Bemba or Nyanja was pitted against any other tribe, it was expected that a non-Bemba or non-Nyanja would not win the day.

If tribe is similar to race, the USA and President Obama provides a compelling illustration of how merit transcends all the subjective categories of human characteristics. For years, the US went by the conception that Blacks were only good at being slaves, house servants and for low-paying jobs. Leadership was never a defining mark of a Black person. This all changed in 2008. And after six, silently but efficacious, years, the US and the world now accept the unpalatable hypothesis that color and race do not define leadership acumen.

In Zambia, the stage is set for the 2015 presidential by-elections in January. The candidates are Hakainde Hichilema – United Party for National Development (UPND); Edgar Lungu – Patriotic Front (PF), and Nevers Mumba – Movement for Multiparty Democracy (MMD). The rest of the political parties, without sacrificing democratic surprises, do not have a chance in the 2015 elections. They may, however, fare better in subsequent elections.

As Zambians are aware, every presidential candidate knows that to become president three factors have to be overcome: Party in power; election rigging and corruption; tribe; and merit and issues. The first two factors ultimately favor the incumbency. That is why it has been very difficult, though not impossible, to unseat a reigning president. For Zambia, fortunately, events such as extreme impoverishment and corruption have enabled Zambians to choose two non-office-holders in both the 1991 and 2011 elections. Is there an earth-shaking event about to take place in 2015 that can upset this unwritten rule?

First, every time a regime in power retained its power, it was relatively healthy and thriving. Kenneth Kaunda (KK) had glued UNIP together under a lurid One-Party system and went on to rule for more than 27 years. Chiluba was thriving under the mantra of the re-introduction of multiparty in Zambia flanked by a magnanimous home empowerment scheme. Mwanawasa rallied under a prosecution of his own mentor, Frederick Chiluba.

Second, the tribal card influenced the majority of outcomes. KK and Chiluba and Michael Sata had a huge

Bemba tribal advantage. Mwanawasa was close to the Bemba, and he was tolerated. Sata was Bemba, and had filled key government positions with his Bemba stalwarts. Although Rupiah Banda was an incumbent, he was up against a staunch Bemba in Michael Sata as we all as a strong corrupt MMD label, and he lost the election.

Third, it is no longer a secret that parties in power rig elections, almost at will. They also use government resources to their advantage. The point in mind is when the *Post* reported in December 2014 that the Lungu-tilted PF ministers (14 out of 19), threatened acting president Guy Scott with dismissal from the party should he refuse to allow Lungu access to the national coffers to fuel his campaign. Scott succumbed, and it is a no brainer – government resources will be used in the 2015 elections.

Fourth, meritorious elections are rare in Zambia. The majority of the people in Zambia (about 60%) are poor. A candidate with access to resources and who promises material things and ministerial and government appointments is ignorantly followed. He or she needs not be brilliant or credible. The reason is simple – the public sector is the largest employer in Zambia. The private sector is weak and does not create ascending jobs for it to be relied upon. People know, explicitly, that a president does not need to be smart or educated or economically savvy; all they need is government resources (because hitherto, no Zambian president has shown alacrity in growing the economy beyond what was inherited from the colonial masters). All that Zambian governments are expert at is redistribution through budgeting (which is confused for a national vision). They forget that any person can set a budget if properly guided.

In 2015, Zambia has a rare opportunity to attempt what has been elusive in years past – choose a president on meritorious grounds. This will mean digging deeper and looking at candidates from issue-based politics, not because of their tribe or party-affiliation. It might mean, for example, looking at Hakainde Hichilema and asking: What does he have that can benefit the nation? And not simply underrating him because he is not Bemba or Nyanja. It might also mean looking at Lungu and Mumba and asking: What do these two people have for Zambia other than incumbency and being a Bemba, respectively?

Meaningful change for Zambia may lie in how intelligent the Zambian electorate answers these illustrious questions. Otherwise, in 2015, Zambia will have new faces in power but not a new economy or new and productive policies.

The moment the ruling party ceases rigging elections through corruption. The moment people choose their president based on merit and not tribe. The moment issues such as how to grow the economy, end poverty and create new and thriving jobs for the masses are prioritized and are not just whims and empty promises. The moment people demand a cogent, clearly-defined and computable vision from their presidential candidates. The moment Zambia votes for a deserved leader – at that moment, Zambian democracy will have graduated from being a growing democracy to a mature democracy.

12 THE UGLY ONES ARE DYING BUT THE BEAUTIFUL ONES ARE STILL NOT YET BORN

[Published: December 22nd, 2014, *Lusaka Times*]

When one read that, "[President] Guy Scott…refused to authorize government financing of the Patriotic Front campaigns, prompting 14 (out of 19) Cabinet ministers to petition for his removal as acting Republican President," it made an interesting read, especially for Africa. African politics, for the most, have epitomized the concept of "Tyranny of the Majority" for decades now. Democracy is usually only paid lip-service to, and the elites rule by connections, kick-backs and corruption.

> THE PRESIDENT IS USUALLY THE CHEERLEADER, WHO CALLS THE SHOTS, AND USING GOVERNMENT RESOURCES AND POWER, DICTATES THROUGH HIS SYCOPHANTS WHEN AND HOW HE EXITS OUT OF POWER.

In Zambia, events of the last few weeks are showing that, after all, the beautiful ones may just be too far from being born. Political thinkers term this uncouth for habit as Neo-Patrimonialism – or the rule by the greedy and the power-hungry.

Here is how it works, and has worked almost unrestrained in Africa: It takes just one-man, so-called president, to rise to power. Under him or her are loyalists, some may call them stalwarts, cadres or any similarly-situated labels. The president anoints a few among the most cantankerous cadres and whom he or she christens as Cabinet ministers (usually, and mostly men, but people who have ascended the pedestal neither due to their acumen nor merit, but through sheer rabblerousing scuffles).

> THE PRESIDENT THEN DRAINS THE NATIONAL COFFERS THROUGH HIS IMPETUOUS MINISTERS (OR PATRONS) AND WHO METICULOUSLY REWARD THEM TO THEMSELVES AND TO THE SYSTEM BOTTOMMOST SOCIAL HIERARCHY – THE CLIENTS. THE CLIENTS THEN DO DAMAGE TO THE OPPOSITION – INSULTING SOME, BEATING UP OTHERS, CAUSING VIOLENCE AND EVEN MURDERING THE UNFORTUNATE.

Those who show allegiance are often compensated with bags of mealie meal, *chitenge* materials or fertilizer, whatever the case may be.

Now you understand what it means when President Scott says, "No more use of government resources." Hate him or love him, this is unheard of among African presidents. Is it the Rubicon crossed already? But just before we begin to resuscitate the diabolical assertions that only White men can save Africa, wait a minute, just wait. Surely Guy Scott is a White African president. It was not his race or color that forced him to take this leap, albeit useful to Zambia. It is the squabbles in the Patriotic Front (PF), and the threat of forcing him to resign the presidency. Not only that Miles Sampa (Scott's preferred candidate) will not be the PF's presidential candidate in the January 2015 presidential by-election. Edgar Lungu's nomination, and perhaps even winning the election, may prompt a political tsunami the nation has never known before. President Scott knows that too well. The Lungu camp also knows that if Sampa becomes the PF strongman, the wrath of Judas will fall on their necks. The stakes were high either way.

The Zambian people have waited, and prayed, for the beautiful ones to be born. And God is saying that the beautiful ones need not be born; the ugly ones just need to die. It should come to the same thing. The only difference is that when the ugly ones are dying, the opposition is also getting topsy-turvy.

> THE PF PARTY, IN ITS CURRENT FORM AND SHAPE, CANNOT DEVELOP ZAMBIA, EVEN IF IT WAS GIVEN ANOTHER 10-YEAR MANDATE. ITS BRAND IS TAINTED WITH CORRUPTION, ABUSE OF NATIONAL RESOURCES, AND LACK OF A COHERENT NATIONAL VISION.

To bring back Zambia to sanity, the PF should be defeated in an election. A clean, sane and new government, untainted with sycophantic scoundrels should then take charge and require a thorough probing of the way the PF have managed national resources, especially during the time President Sata was incapacitated. If the opposition front in Zambia were a force to reckon with, one of these two, either Hakainde Hichilema or Nevers Mumba would be president in

Zambia come January 2015. If the opposition fails to take this chance, the PF will destroy the country, not because it will win the elections, but because if it does, vengeance, and not goodwill, will rule Zambia for the next few months. And the result will be, of course, the same old, dirty, unsanitary, poverty-stricken and hopeless nation.

13 LET JUSTICE BE DONE THOUGH THE HEAVENS FALL

[Published: February 16th, 2015, *Lusaka Times*]

The politics of the motherland have been interesting. But the politicians are systematically undermining the Rule of Law and whirling the Judiciary into rebel extravaganza. The arrest of Mutembo Nchito, the current Director of Public Prosecution (DPP) of Zambia, is turning Zambia perfunctorily into the reserves of zoo politics arbitrating jungle justice. If one is a stranger to the politics of the land they would think the Latin maxim of *fiat justitia ruat caelum* (or "Let justice be done though the heavens fall") is taking root.

They would have ample references to July 16th, 2002, when the Zambian Parliament lifted late President Chiluba's immunity. They would also refer to March 15th, 2013, just over ten years after the fact, when President

Michael Sata's Patriotic Front (PF) lifted former President Rupiah Banda's immunity as well. The paradox is, however, that in both events the name of Mutembo Nchito was not remotely in association.

Was Mutembo Nchito a political whip who after his job is done is now being discarded? It was just after the 2001 presidential elections. Mwanawasa was the new sheriff in town, and to help him perform his job of law and order, the Nchitos were his easy choice. It all started with a betrayal. Mwanawasa graced his Tusk Force prosecution team with the Nchito Brothers, as they were called. This did not, definitely, go well with the then DPP, the late Mukelabai Mukelabai.

In fact, Mukelabai had dismissed Mutembo Nchito from prosecuting Richard Sakala's case, but Mwanawasa overruled contrary to Article 56 of the *Zambian Constitution*. By law, Mutembo Nchito had no mandate to prosecute on behalf of the Zambian government, it was alleged, because he was a private corporate lawyer. Mutembo Nchito himself became ratified as DPP under very disconcerting circumstances to replace Chalwe Mchenga, now a judge. Subsequently, Nchito became involved in all major cases backed by the government.

Zambia has not made political and economic progress because the same people have dominated public life for years. These same people keep making the same decisions, or lack thereof, which have taken the nation nowhere. There seems to be a curse of recycled manpower hovering above the Zambian panoply. Because it is the same people who make decisions that affect the nation, vengeance and vendetta loom large. In fact, it seems the entire saga has its genesis in Kenneth Kaunda animosity against Frederick Chiluba. Kaunda, conveniently using the instruments of power at his disposal such as a One-Party State, the *Public Order Act* and hijacking of all parastatal bosses as the "boss of bosses," and etc., meted out on all his political "opponents" with vengeful venom. He maintained this kind of rule for 27 years. When Chiluba became president, he retaliated. His detention without trial under Kaunda was rewarded with detaining Kaunda on UFO allegations.

Then it was Mwanawasa. Fearing, with the help of Mutembo Nchito to some extent, that his "cabbage" tag would rub frenetically on his government initiated a precedential immunity lifting politics. (Zambia is the only country in the 21st century to have lifted the immunity of its presidents twice – which is a shameful heirloom by itself). Sata was not any different from his predecessors; he targeted Rupiah Banda. The former president's case is technically alive in courts. Banda himself is not immune from the politics of vengeance, either. In January 2015, he did the unthinkable. He ditched the MMD party under which he ruled Zambia for three years and joined the PF party that defeated him just because he wanted to run away from prosecution from corruption and abuse of office allegations. President Lungu will be out of his mind to now let Banda go free. If President Lungu does otherwise, that would be the biggest betrayal of the Zambian people's trust, ever.

Awful as this might seem, the targeting of Mutembo Nchito is the lowest the Zambian government has come to on its integrity index. As stated above, Nchito's DPP job had been controversial from the beginning. In some respect, some would be glad he is arrested. However, in a country that prides in the Rule of Law, the motivation cannot be this malicious. Just as in the appointment of the former chief electoral officer of the just-ended presidential by-election, Justice Mambilima, as Chief Justice of Zambia, President Lungu can do better to show leadership judgment, in the attempted arrest of Nchito the PF government is again pontificating the rule of vengeful men. Newton Ng'uni has argued that he has a duty as a Zambian citizen to ensuring that laws are observed and respected by all regardless of their status in society. But this is fickle. Ng'uni is a former Finance Deputy Minister. Why is it that somehow under Mwanawasa and Sata Nchito was a saint and he has just turned into a demon now? And Nchito is not innocent, too. He is on record now trying to accuse the police of arresting people found loitering at night. He has now suddenly learned it is against people's economic rights and freedoms. He did not voice out for the people before the Lungu administration came into power.

My dear countrymen, it is important for Zambia to understand four things. First, that the whole is always bigger than the sum of its aggregate parts. For over twenty years, the same people who have run Zambia have taken sane and vulnerable people for a ride. They assign each other to offices arbitrarily and they rule without any ideas for national transformation. They interpret the law to suit their own whims and caprices. They choose to obey some laws and disobey others. They change ministerial positions like undergarments. They vacillate from policy to policy like shifting shadows. They are not stable like weather. And at the end of the day, they come back to the electorate with the same lies expecting to be elected to the positions which only fatten their own bellies and not those of the children in the street or of the senior citizens in the villages. They are political chameleons who change party colors at will and subscribe to the politics of poverty. Does Zambia really need these kinds of people to rule?

Second, no matter what the motive is, the government should not be above the law. A DPP is a Constitutional office. The person who occupies that office enjoys tenure regardless of how he was appointed and ratified. Contrary to Article 58 of the *Zambian Constitution*, a DPP can only be removed from office for incompetency or incapacity, neither of which applies to Nchito. If this witch-hunt succeeds, it will undermine both the Constitution (which is the highest law of the land) and the will of the people. Tyranny of the majority and the majority of one, both do not have a place in democratic societies. If government or its stooges are allowed to abuse their powers by arbitrarily and unilaterally sanctioning removal of democratically constructed personnel from their positions, Zambia will begin to lose a grip on the fundamentals of modern political management and may be a liability in the community of nations.

Third, Zambian politicians should adhere strictly to the moral law of tolerance and love under God. As a Christian Nation, Zambia should be the best place on earth where people should be valued for who they are and given respect as citizens. When will Zambia begin a path towards healing rather than killing? When will the government begin to end the politics of vengeance and substitute it with one of penitence? When will ruling parties cease from using power as a means to settle political scores? I vouch that until the nation becomes a balm, its economic conditions will never retain calm. Unless we rise above hatred and revenge, law will be just a weapon in the hands of a government with legitimate power but with illegitimate ideas.

Fourth and last, where is President Lungu's promise

to the people that he would perpetrate what Sata began? When it was argued that he had no campaign platform, he said he would continue where Sata left. Now it is clear that he is undoing, and not continuing, what Sata started. For example, in his appointments, his position on mining and tax and his attempted arrest of Nchito, to mention but a few. Mr. President, is this continuing the legacy of President Sata or it is just too early to call? Zambians should be wise and demand that justice is done though the heavens should fall.

14 MUGABE-KIBAKI SIGNATURE

[Published between January 2007 and December 2008]

The story of democracy in Africa is one of special interest to all concerned, especially to those who desire a better Africa. Unlike India or the United States of America, African democracy has a recent history. In fact our transition is still in its latest phases. And yet, signs rarely cheat. What we see today has the propensity to define what lies ahead. Recent events in Kenya and Zimbabwe only serve to indicate the lack of progress in our transition to democracy. Mugabe and Mwai Kibaki epitomize the old-style authoritarianism, sort of popular authoritarianism gone awry.

Mugabe is a kind of a right-wing authoritarian, the kind who bases their rule on vendetta. But in the process of his person vengeance and a fear of what would happen to him, cramps power in his bosom at every cost.

Mugabe's rule can amply be described as economic failure, political confusion and democratically malaise. In Zimbabwe, unlike in most right-wing authoritarian nations, neither economic development nor liberal political liberty is encouraged.

Mwai Kibaki came to power through an election. In Kibaki, we find a modern concept of democracy in Africa playing the same codes as the old concepts of authoritarianism. At the end of the Second World War, most countries were trying to define their political future based on ideology. Some called for radical social transformations and revolutions. They opted for a utopia, a perfect world of supreme laws, no wars and *laissez faire* economic principles. This, however, did not result in exactly what was anticipated. Socialism and Communism emerged. Communist governments desired to plan their economies, own property in common, and ensure equality of results. They also put faith in human perfection. But they deemed the free market economy as being unfair.

In Search of a Political Culture

Karl Marx and Engels went further and developed what they called a theory of Scientific Socialism. They believed that the world economy is the history of economic ownership. They postulated that whoever owned the means of production such as lands also controlled the political machinery. They abhorred the people they called capitalists, who they believed would be overthrown by the proletariat or the working class. They created an impression that workers were sort of alienated from the economic activities of their nations. Marx and

Engel's faith in the rise of the proletariat did not happen in their time or as they hoped. But the events of the October Revolution in 1917 of the Bolshevik Party in Russia sort of vindicated their hypothesis. In that year Lenin took control of the new government that had replaced the Czarist regime months earlier. However, the faithful followers of Marx were soon to be disgruntled by Marxist-Leninism. Initially, Marx had hinted that the role of the revolutionary party would only be to control the state until such a time as the masses would be ready to embrace Communism, a society where every means of production would be held in common. Lenin had become a dictator, an extreme totalitarian.

With the fall of the Berlin Wall in 1991 also came the end of the Cold War. Most nations which were under the Soviet rule began to look to liberal democracy as the most formidable means of government. The result was the birth of non-revolutionary movements in most parts of the world. These new trends were committed to upholding the Constitution, open doors to multiparty politics, and accept free market policies. Africa played a key role in the democratization process in the early 1960s. The decolonization of most African states at this time was a clear indication that Africa was ready to embrace sovereign status and self-rule. This followed immediately after the Portuguese Revolution in 1974.

Democratic-Minded Leadership

The moves from authoritarianism and totalitarianism to democracy were very important steps towards enhancement of freedom in Africa. Africa fought hard, even sacrificing its blood to gain political emancipation.

The vision of the freedom fighters and nationalists of the time was for a sovereign and self-determined Africa. This was partly to be realized through African leadership. The eras of Nazism, Stalinism, the politicization of society, and control of the media, education, the press, and communication was to be the thing of the past. Slowly but surely, this new African leadership were to pave a way for democracy.

After roughly forty years of self-rule, we are still to ask: Are we ready for democracy in Africa? Going by the developments in Keya in January and in Zimbabwe in April, the answer to that question is no. But Kenya and Zimbabwe alone cannot decide the determination of most African states to democratize. That is the hope we still have for Africa. It lies, to the larger extent, in the rising of what I prefer to call Emerging African Leadership. These leaders will first and foremost have to understand the signs of a mature democratic society.

Benchmarks for Democratic Progress

There are three indicators of democratic progress anywhere in the world. The first of these indicators is a political culture. When a large number of people begin to value the substance of human rights, equality, and self-government, they are advancing in the understanding of democratic ideals. Democracy thrives where the culture for democratic enhancement is encouraged. There can never be a functional democracy unless there is a political culture to sustain it. A culture of tolerance, political and electoral fairness, equality of laws, the rule of law and the protection of fundamental human rights and freedoms enshrined in the Constitution. Judging from Mugabe and

Kibaki it is quite obvious that we have progressed from this initial test with some wounds. In Zambia in the 2001 elections the incumbent wanted to change the Constitution and run for a third term in office. In 2007, we sort of saw signs of that as well. Although for the most part, African states have made tremendous progress on the transfer of power, a lot still remains to be done.

The second indicator is the strength of the civil society. In a functional democracy, the people should have the desire to participate in civic activities. Democracy is strengthened when people join the civil society and participate in the democratic process of their nations. This helps to decentralize power and make government more accountable. A nation with a weak civil society is devoid of fair play. Non-Governmental Organizations (NGOs), interest groups and the Church act as a direct check on the activities of government. But they do more than that, they also supplement government effort and circumvent red tape and bureaucratic barriers in serving people's needs. They also act as a voice for the voiceless and provide awareness to needy areas through advocacy and lobby.

Thirdly, there is a correlation between democracy and economic development. There is some truth that nations that embrace democratic tendencies also tend to favor the market economy and free enterprise. History has proven that democracy empowers people to think independently and productively. Most industrialized countries are also countries which enjoy improved standards of living and higher rates of employment. Most of these countries also embrace liberal democratic ideals. China is the exception, but recently China has opened doors to a free-market economy which is reminiscent of democracy.

Emerging African Leadership

Africa faces enormous challenges in its transition to democracy. The political culture of free and fair elections, as demonstrated by the elections in Zimbabwe and Kenya recently, is still shaky and weak. Most countries south of the Sahara are ranked among the poorest nations of the world. Most of this poverty is artificial, caused by instabilities and displacements in the war-torn regions of Africa. Some of it is due to poor planning, and historic mismanagement. The huge burden, however, lies in the future on the emerging African leadership. And democracy will hugely play a key role in the economic development of Africa.

15 MUGABE: HEARTLESS DEMAGOGUE OR CREATURE OF IMPERIAL AVARICE?

[Written in June 2008]

On June 1st, 2008, President Robert Mugabe was in the Italian capital for an important UN world food conference which was held in response to soaring prices and the growing demand for food. Despite facing a presidential run-off against opposition leader Morgan Tsvangirai later this month, he took several days out there in Rome with his wife and a small coterie of officials. The European Union has a longstanding travel ban on the veteran leader but he was allowed to attend UN Global Food Summit. The Food and Agriculture Organization of the United Nations (FAO) that was hosting the summit said all member countries were invited and that it was at the discretion of each member state who they decide to send. And Zimbabwe sent President Mugabe.

Which View?

Nations deal with international relations according to which view they hold. Two most common are the Liberal and the Realist views. Liberals believe in the role of general morality in dealing with global relations. They basically believe that cooperation among nations is possible because of shared international values and the common desire for cooperation.

Realists, on the other hand, are of the view that cooperation is not possible because of nations' differing interests. According to this view people seek to advance only causes that have their nation's interest at heart. Thus, nations may label those countries which do not agree with their international agenda as terrorists or undemocratic, depending on their view of that nation or its leaders.

The Western View of Mugabe

Perhaps the best view of the Western-mindset on Mugabe is what Jim Anderson said: "He took over a country that was renowned as the breadbasket of Africa and now...he's got millions of people virtually starving." Anderson believes Mugabe's economic policies have plunged his country into 165,000% inflation. Or have they? When you read the news about Mugabe what comes out is always a picture of a man without a heart for his people, a leader out of touch with the economic realities of his suffering people. That is a Realist view; it always lays blame on someone else. Notably, Mugabe has made some blunders in the way he reallocated farmlands from the White farmers in Zimbabwe. But the reaction of the West has not been moral considering the number of innocent Zimbabweans that have suffered due to sanctions imposed upon Zimbabwe.

The Real Issue

There is always a huge disparity in the way the media, especially the Western-backed media, reports on African affairs. What makes news about Africa is predictable: there must be a coup, extreme hunger or poverty or HIV/AIDS or something misfortunate. But when something conflicts directly against the Western interests, it will capture global headlines. And Mugabe happens to fall into this latter category. The real issue why the West is fuming over Mugabe is not what Anderson asserts. The fact is most African countries are not at the same level economically as they were at independence. And there are reasons to that which are beyond the scope of this article.

Mugabe puts it straight forward why the West is treating him the way it is. He believes it is in retaliation to what he calls "the measures we took": "In retaliation for the measures we took to empower the Black majority, the United Kingdom has mobilized friends and allies in Europe, North America, Australia, and New Zealand to impose illegal economic sanctions against Zimbabwe."

The truth is Great Britain was enraged by Mugabe's land redistribution policy. The fact that Zimbabweans should be empowered to own land raises no question to me. How Mugabe did it perhaps has more questions than answers. Whatever the case, Mugabe's actions stepped on Britain's interests in Zimbabwe. If the West seriously desired to punish Mugabe, it should not have been by imposing economic sanctions. Because when that is done, it is not Mugabe who suffers; it is the hopeless women and children of Zimbabwe. In this way alone, Britain and its allies were wrong.

Westphalian Model

According to international law, all nations are equal. By the 1648 Treaty of Westphalia, nation-states agreed to treat each other equal as nations, and not according to power or economic status. In this regard, Zimbabwe or any African nation is as equal to Britain as Britain is to the United States of America. As a sovereign nation, Zimbabwe has every right to decide what it wants to do with its land, albeit, in a humane and rational way. But even if Mugabe made a fatal error of judgment, his decision was made as of a sovereign state, just as the USA made a decision to invade Iraq or Cecil Rhodes to plunder South Africa.

Africa Should Learn to Read between the Lines

In Africa, we stand limp on one leg; we have no news. Everything we know is told to us from one perspective. If someone says Mugabe is bad and Tsvangirai is good, we believe. But who is saying so? What we know for sure is that Mugabe has made some serious errors, and he continues to make them. But what we don't know is what Tsvangirai will do or who is behind or funding his campaigns. It might turn out to be bittersweet; keep Mugabe in power and exacerbate Zimbabwe's already ravaged economy. Or elect Tsvangirai, and hand the whole country into the hands of imperialist.

If Africa is going to develop, it must learn to stand its grounds on certain issues, especially on those issues that border on sovereignty. History has taught us one lesson: Resources leave Africa and don't come back. History has also taught us that those who claim to invest in Africa have not made us better. And the bitter truth is that even our progress is not recognized. Zambia, for example, has conducted very successful elections, and transferred power successively in peaceful and democratic fashions. But who cares to make it an international news item?

The fact of the matter is the sanctions imposed on Zimbabwe by Britain's allies are immoral and uncalled for. The people of Zimbabwe have lost their dignity and are dying of hunger because of Mugabe? I don't think so. It is because of someone's revenge. Mugabe confiscated land from White Zimbabwean farmers, and not from the Americans, Australians or New Zealanders. If there is a nation Zimbabwe should not trade with, it should be Great Britain. But why should the rest of the world deny the innocent Zimbabweans their livelihood because London has conflicts with Mugabe?

African Ubuntu is Anti-Xenophobia

Recently 55 people died in South Africa in a xenophobic escapade. And everyone else is lambasting the South Africans for the incident. But people are not trying to make a connection between the elections in Zimbabwe, the travel of Tsvangirai to South Africa, and the unfortunate killing in the xenophobia. South Africans have never wanted foreigners to leave their land; Mandela made it very clear at inaugural. The group that did this is correctly called a gang, sort of an organized force. And the manner in which it did the killings tells its own story. But it is the timing and the motive that CNN or the BBC will not report. In Bemba they say: "*Insofu ngashalwa ichani echichulilamo*" (Literally: when the elephants fight; the grass suffers).

In the past Africans were less educated and less travelled. The books they read were written for them, many times from a Westernized perspective. Africans lived on imported ideas, beliefs and even culture. As the years have passed that *Ubuntu* that defined Africans as a unique and distinct people faded away. Africans nearly began to doubt who they were any more. But now things are changing; Africans are starting to believe they are competent and capable. Most Africans now are decently educated and are highly travelled. They are beginning to redefine who they are and are competing favorably on any challenge with others.

Given this scenario, it will not be surprising that in the near future, Africans will assert their sovereignty and marshal unprecedented competitive advantage in global affairs. They will learn to be their own masters and not small puppets dancing to the *be-us* songs of neo-imperialism. By then the Mugabe-type leaders who play politics of vengeance will vanish, and the Tsvangirai-type leaders who stand on one leg will give way to a new breed of African leadership - a leadership weaned off slave-mentality, colonial ignominy and economic plunderism.

> Oh, the mighty,
> how they have conspired against the weak!
> And the weaker have fallen,
> Almost annihilated from the face of the earth!
> Who will speak for the weak?
> Tell me, who will?

16 GENOCIDE IN DARFUR

[Written between January 2008 and June 2017]

A swine flu (H1N1) is eminent according to WHO's Director General, Dr. Margaret Chan,[31] who has raised the alert levels to five. The H1N1 outbreak is threatening the whole world. In Mexico, the

---

[31] Since May 2017, Dr Tedros Adhanom Ghebreyesus is WHO's Director-General

epicenter of the disease, nearly 160 people have died so far. Over sixty cases and one fatality have been reported in the US, thirteen cases in Canada, and a growing number of cases in Europe.

The media is all over this, and world bodies ranging from the United Nations (UN) to the World Health Organization (WHO) to the European Union (EU), are on their toes to issuing both warning statements and providing the populous with more preventive information about a potential pandemic. President Barack Obama on Monday, April 29th, 2009, issued a cautious warning saying, "Although the situation is a source of concern, there is no need to panic."

Meanwhile as all this myriad of information, warnings, preparedness and preventive and curative activities and measures are taking place, Mia Farrow, a renowned actor, appeared on CNN Larry King Live. She was being interviewed about a sixteen-day hunger strike she has commenced. She is fasting in order to raise awareness about the atrocities and genocide going on in Darfur, Sudan.

Media reports estimate that since the conflict began in February 2003, about 450,000 people have been killed, and three million people have been displaced. All this is taking place in one country on earth. If there are still critics there who still deny that what is taking place in Darfur is not a genocide, let them only see what a swine flu that has not even claimed 0.1 percent of victims is causing alarm and panic in the Western World.

Tear of God

If there is one thing that has yet to be thoroughly

addressed, it is the difference between being human and only people. Centuries ago, some human races were not even people. Through the UN and other organizations, the word human is slowly coming into the global vocabulary. But now it remains to be seen if other humans are more human than others, especially when such other humans live on a continent called Africa.

The UN has admitted its error in Rwanda when it did not intervene militarily as the Tutsis and Hutus massacred each other in the Rwandese genocide. "Western powers bear criminal responsibility for Rwanda's 1994 genocide because they did not attempt to stop it," said General Romeo Dallaire, the Canadian commander of the UN peacekeeping force in Rwanda at the time of the genocide. When you watch the movie, *Hotel Rwanda*, starring Don Cheadle, you cannot but shed a tear of God because of how the UN failed a people.

Responsibility to Protect

Nations have fashioned means and ways to protect their territories from external threats and dangers. Through collective defence, such organizations as the North Atlantic Treaty Organization (NATO) have ramped up resources to defend their member states from threats. Collective defence may give way to collective security where one member within the ambit of collective defence poses a threat to other member states.

As far as collective security is concerned, other members may commit themselves to and even join forces in an alliance against a member state that threatens the peace. The quintessential and modern epitome of such collective security has been demonstrated by the UN. In order to effectively provide collective security, the UN and now such organizations as the African Union (AU) carry out peacekeeping missions in defaulting and warring regions.

Peacekeeping usually involve provision of a force or forces that monitor ceasefires and may serve as buffers between the combatants. Because a peacekeeping force is only there with the consent of the combatants, its role is limited to that of "keeping the peace' and may resort to force only in self-defence. This is what differentiates peacekeeping from peacemaking.

Initially, collective security only involved intervention in inter-state conflicts. Recently, the UN has expanded its mission to intervene in intra-state conflicts such as in civil wars, separatist conflicts, genocide campaigns, and humanitarian emergencies. With this expanded mandate the UN has been able to intervene and end civil wars and conflicts in trouble-torn regions.

This shift has mainly been necessitated by a doctrine of Responsibility to Protect (R2P). The R2P principles were first developed by the International Commission on Intervention and State Sovereignty (ICISS). ICISS was established by the Canadian government in 2001.

The central theme of the doctrine of R2P is enshrined in the truth that all people have a right to be protected from serious harm or threat of destruction. The traditional idea has been that sovereign states should be free from outside interference by other states. But the international community faces no more critical issue currently than how to protect people caught in new and large-scale humanitarian crises. R2P doctrine proposes a legal and ethical basis for humanitarian intervention preferably through the UN in a state that is unwilling to prevent genocides, massive killings, and other massive human rights violations.

Humanitarian intervention has been controversial both when it has happened, as in Kosovo, and when it has failed to happen, as in Rwanda. While there is general agreement internationally that we should not stand by in the face of massive violations of human rights, respect for the sovereign rights of states maintains a central place among the principles governing relations between states.

With this controversy also comes even more controversy that the UN will only exercise R2P when the interests of its most powerful members are concerned. These members are usually from the Northern Hemisphere. Whether it a question of swine flu or terrorist attack, when it directly affects the powerful nations the UN pulls all its resources and intervenes. Somehow this is understood as most of these powerful nations are the very nations that contribute more in monetary terms.

However, if the world is going to be a safer place and if the threat of war and disease is going to be brought to a minimum, there should be concerted effort by both the Western nations and the UN to intervene with the same sense of urgency regardless of where the conflicts happen or where disease breaks out.

When it comes to maintaining world peace or keeping the world free from sickness and disease, self-interest will not win the day. Disease, terrorism and wars affect all of us equally, whether we are victims or victors. Listening to Wolf Blitzer's the Situation Room on April 27th, 2009; I noticed how excited some commentators were when questioned why the swine flu seems to be fatal in Mexico and mild in the US at that time.

One commentator alluded to the fact that the US has a superior health-care system to that of Mexico. While that fact is unarguably correct, it is such attitudes that potentially harm world peace. This type of thinking leads to abysmal reactions when atrocities are being perpetrated in one corner of the world rather than in the other.

In 1999, the NATO intervened militarily in Kosovo. The UN Security Council approved this intervention after the fact. This also is simple to understand. The Security Council comprises the same members that form the core of NATO, with the exception of China and Russia.

In 2003, the US declared war on Iraq. The Iraq War would not qualify as either a collective operation or as a peacekeeping operation. The US used its military, economic and political leverage to override the Security Council and declare war on Iraq.

In the name of "civilizing" and "democratizing" Iraq, both Bush presidents had invaded a sovereign nation. If this had happened with a less developed nation or with a poor nation, such a nation would be treated differently, and perhaps even be labeled a terrorist regime or failed state. Self-interest, idiosyncratically, try to paint the activities of other nations as evil or more tenuous while the same activities, if they were done by a strong and powerful nation, may be justified as acceptable, and even necessary.

This approach may explain why when General Romeo Dallaire, the commander of the international force, was asked to intervene militarily in one of recent history's worst genocides in Rwanda, and his reply coerced on him by the UN was, "We are peacekeepers, not peacemakers." The sad result of this double standard was the massacre of some two or more million Hutus in Rwanda.

Hotel Rwanda is an epigrammatic illustration of the hypocrisy of the international community in the way it reacts to conflict resolution or disease outbreaks in different parts of the world. This failure of the international community to protect the Rwandese people from themselves leading to the 1994 genocide should be a lesson to what is happening in Darfur.

R2P is inevitable if the world is going to overcome corrupt and selfish regimes. The case in question is that of Myanmar. In 2008, Myanmar, a country officially known as Burma was ravaged by a strong cyclone that destroyed property and killed thousands of people. The military junta which ruled the island opposed international humanitarian intervention. Thousands more people died due to the political naivety of the junta.

Omar al-Bashir

Al-Bashir, who came to power in 1989 through a bloodless military coup that ousted the government of Prime Minister Sadiq al-Mahdi, negotiated an end to the Second Sudanese Civil War in October 2004. This civil war was one of the longest-running and deadliest wars of the 20th century.

Since then, however, there has been a violent conflict in Darfur. During his presidency, there have been several violent struggles between the Janjaweed militia and rebel groups such as the Sudan People's Liberation Army (SPLA), Sudanese Liberation Army (SLA) and the Justice and Equality Movement (JEM). Guerilla warfare among these groups has been waged in the Darfur region. Due to this civil war, three million people are being displaced, and diplomatic relations between Sudan and Chad have been in a crisis.

In July 2008, the prosecutor of the International Criminal Court (ICC), Luis Moreno-Ocampo, accused al-Bashir of genocide, crimes against humanity and war crimes in Darfur. The court issued an arrest warrant for al-Bashir on March 4th, 2009, on counts of war crimes and crimes against humanity, but ruled that there was insufficient evidence to prosecute him for genocide. The warrant is expected to be delivered to the Sudanese government, which is unlikely to execute it.

There is controversy surrounding the issuance of an arrest of warrant on al-Bashir. Some nations and bodies that oppose this look at it as immoral to indict a sitting head of state and a presidential candidate in the first democratic election with multiple political parties participating in nine years. Among such nations and bodies that oppose this indictment are Russia and China, the AU, League of Arab States (LAS), and the Non-Aligned Movement (NAM).

The Right Response

When it comes to genocides, any response that is in the interest of justice is the right response. The indictment of al-Bashir, from the international community point of view, is a sign of a paradigm shift. In the seventeenth century, Western Europe would perhaps indicate that Africans deserved to kill each other. In 1994, the West would have cited peacekeeping and not peacemaking as its mission in conflict regions. But in 2008 and 2009, the ICC takes a step that is not only welcome but an indication of good things to come.

Those who oppose this should learn from history. For

the first time in the history of international justice, the UN and the West have taken a stand that is both moral and just on behalf of an African state. By indicting al-Bashir, albeit, on war crimes and crimes against humanity, but not on genocide, a powerful signal has been sent that self-interest is slowly giving way to equitability.

What is happening in Darfur constitutes genocide. If nothing is done the almost half a million human beings who have died may reach a million and more. The UN, EU and the AU should not only issue a warrant of arrest for Omar al-Bashir, but should do what was done in 1999 and 2003 in Kosovo and Iraq, respectively.

In the past, the international community did not consider African states because these states were of less strategic importance. But events in Iraq, Afghanistan, Sri-Lanka, Pakistan, Gaza and the Mediterranean Sea, are changing how the so-called less strategic nations are viewed today. Whether it is the acts of pirates in the Somalian waters or the Taliban in the Pakistani mountains, the effects ripple through to threaten even peaceful nations.

Still, more needs to be done by both the UN and the West. The H1N1 outbreak should give us a clue to how close the UN and the West has come to breaking the self-interest barrier. But it should do even more; it should show a consistence in the way the UN and the West may react if, and only if, the H1N1 should reach the African continent. We are blessed in North America and Europe with competent medical personnel and facilities, and strong healthcare systems. The same cannot be said of Africa.

Currently, H1N1 is only wreaking havoc on North America and Europe, and the response has been swift and coordinated. If the H1N1 should reach Africa, God forbid, we should expect to see the same response. This, together with the manner in which the West will respond next to the genocide in Darfur, should either give us hope or cause for concern as to the plight of the developing nations. Meanwhile, we pray that this outbreak should eventually diminish or die altogether.

17 ALIENOPHOBIA: A CHALLENGE TO CIVILIZED NATIONS

[Published: March 30th, 2019, *Lusaka Times, Mackrack*]

In the 1990s, I resided in the area in Lusaka, Zambia's Capital, in the flats (apartment buildings) previously occupied by the leaders of the South Africa African National Congress (ANC). It is believed that all the giants of South African political struggles, including Thabo Mbeki, Jacob Zuma, Nelson Mandela, and many icons took refuge there at some point. Zambia and other African countries generously helped, sometimes with their own blood, to free South Africa from Apartheid brutality.

Why are we today reading and witnessing a blatant lack of gratitude from the Black South African government of Matamela Cyril Ramaphosa? When President Ramaphosa succeeded Jacob Zuma in 2018, he was hailed as a savior. He had vowed to work for the ordinary citizen, root out the country's corruption and curb the gaping inequality that continue to infuriate millions of South Africans. Now, the president seems to be sanctioning a form of debilitating xenophobia I can only dub, "alienophobia," or a deluded fear of, and subsequent termination of Black foreigners in South Africa.

Disgruntled South Africans blame foreigners or "Kwerekweres" for their miseries. They want to violently attack and kill any Kwerekwere who fails to leave South Africa by May 13th, 2019 (culminating into the Monday after the elections on May 8th, 2019). Like the White Supremacists in USA, the Alienphobes believe that the foreigners are responsible for their poverty and lack of employment. This cannot be too, too far from the truth. It is a clear disregard and willful blindness to the history of South Africa. And it is not my intention to re-lecture South Africans about their own history. It is, however, important to learn from general African history, in terms of genocides and violence.

We all remember the genocide in Rwanda. The Rwandan genocide by the Hutu majority government between April and July 1994 was a blood-bath, a brutal slaughter of the Tutsis in Rwanda during the 1990s Rwandan Civil War. In that slaughter, within three months, close to one million people were murdered. This was while the world watched. Both the UN and OAU (currently African Union – AU) were flatly impotent. African nations watched, and so did the West. No matter the excuse or justification, the world let the Tutsis down.

We cannot overlook or ignore what is brewing underneath South Africa. Hate is blind to reason. The South African government should not only protect foreigners from the hooligans, but also under international law, the nation has an obligation to do so. Where the South African government fails its duty, the UN should exercise its Responsibility to Protect (R2P) mandate. The regional organizations in Africa as well as the AU should speak out directly and strongly against the pending atrocities of innocent foreigners in South Africa.

President Ramaphosa may easily win the re-election, but at what expense. Ramaphosa understands better what Nelson Mandela did and stood for. The president should not sacrifice principle for blood. He should stand up for the Black people of Africa resident in South Africa. These are the people who sold him cattle and made him rich. These are the people who sacrificed to liberate South Africa from Apartheid.

18 XENOPHOBIA: HAPPENING IN SOUTH AFRICA

[Written in May 2008]

Forty-two people were killed [on May 23rd, 2008] in South Africa. Hundreds have been displaced. A gang of people claim foreigners are taking their jobs and causing violence in South Africa. President Thabo Mbeki has responded promptly with police deployment and he should be commended. What is disturbing is that this sort of thing is happening in South Africa which few years ago sought refuge in different countries as a result of apartheid in that country. But what is appalling is that in this time and age such an awful thing is happening.

By definition xenophobia is dislike or fear of people from other countries. This is what is happening in Johannesburg, South Africa. Xenophobia, like racism, racial discrimination, and related intolerances, is an infringement on human rights. Foreigners, regardless of how they entered into a country, have protected human rights. The United Nations Universal Declaration of Human Rights states in Article 28: "Everyone is entitled to a social and international order in which the rights and freedoms set forth in this Declaration can be fully realized." In South Africa, as in every other country, foreigners are protected from attack, abuse and discrimination.

I mentioned that it is disturbing that such thing is happening in South Africa. First, South Africa should know better after years of oppression by the apartheid regime. South Africans, including Mandela and Mbeki, found refuge as foreigners in other countries. As foreigners in other countries, these South African leaders planned the liberation of South Africa which these gangs are enjoying today.

Second, it is barely seven years ago when a conference against xenophobia was held right in South Africa. From August 31st to September 7th, 2001, a "World Conference against Racism, Racial Discrimination, Xenophobia and Related Intolerance" was held in Durban, South Africa. At this conference Africa demanded an apology from major European and North American countries from slavery and xenophobia. Then we demanded an apology but today we are doing the same thing.

This is unacceptable, and those people who killed the forty-two victims should be answerable before the law. The South African government should apologize to the victims' families and immediately compensate all those affected.

19 OMS RULE IN CHINA
- AFRICA SHOULD BE WORRIED

[Published: March 9th, 2018, *AllAfrica, Pambazuka, Muckrack*]

Power is sweet, even unavoidable, at times. Call him president, commander-in-chief, head of the security council, party chief, and chairman of everything from innocuous intra-governmental agencies to multi-lateral conglomerates baptized into China's mainstream socialistic agenda; may be brewing a cocktail too detrimental to the future of democracy in Africa.

Since the Fall of the Berlin Wall, and in effect the dismantling of the Iron Curtain in the early 1990s that pitted the West against the East, the last of the strong men in Africa had almost collapsed. Zimbabwe and Uganda yielded their adamancy until 2018 when Mugabe was silently deposed. Now, and not unusual, Uganda's Museveni is demanding a forever regime. Next, it will be South Africa, then Nigeria and finally Zambia. Strong men are not a new phenomenon; they predate the collapse of Colonialism and outlive empire building. They are as old as monarchical ceremonialism in United Kingdom and monarchical internalism in Lesotho. In all these forms, strong men government was not a threat to world economic and political equilibrium. Until now.

There are three reasons why we should be worried of the new surge in One-Man Strong Rule (OMS Rule). The rise of China; the democratic naivety under Trump in the US; and the inevitable catalyst for Africa.

First, China is rising, and with it the enshrining into its Constitution of the all-mighty-for-life presidency for Xi. By the new Constitutional dictates, Xi has been conferred upon such enormous levels of ideological authority that he is to be only equal to Mao Zedong. The New Era so-donned, will empower Xi with "Xi Jinping Thought on Socialism with Chinese Characteristics for a New Era." Camouflaged into these so-called glorious words is OMS Rule. Xi will be the undisputed one-man ruler of China – controlling everything from economic forays to thought and reason. Thought and reason are the last to fall. When they do as the case in China now, freedom can permanently wave bye-bye!

China has already penetrated most major economies of the world through its products and services. There is no world trade without Chinese advantage. China is everywhere, any time and in any form. But China had resisted ideological domination or should I put it, had its ideological momentum curtailed due to America's policing in yester-years. However, with the weakening of American democracy internally under Trump, Xi and China have finally found their inner energy to emerge. And BIG China will emerge.

Second, US has been weakened internally by the Trumpistic policies to mitigate over China's rising. This is, perhaps one of the greatest defining marks on world politics. Hitherto, the US kept the world sane by preaching, though not always practicing, democratic ideals. To that end, the world found a level of political equalization. Small countries had an olive branch to institute democratic standards and be guided by the Rule of Law (and not of a man). But with this internal moral and political erosion in the US, China will scintillate its own sparkle, and countries, especially in Africa, will again be tempted to return to the vomitus – to the politics of single party dictatorships. Unless America returns to its guardianship of the democratic diadem, there will be no end to which OMS Rule will not scale.

Last, Africa will, again and sadly, be the culprit. Mark my words, it is already happening in Africa. Uganda's ruling party is pushing for a referendum that could extent President Yoweri Museveni's rule to 2035. This is in spite of the fact that the opposition parties have objected. And for a good reason – because this will be a declaration of life presidency for the incumbent who has been president since 1986. Uganda's ruling party will then justify its course of action by citing Xi and the Chinese model. Where is the US, and with it the rest of us (no pun intended!)?

The demerits of the OMS Rule are intractable. In the least, they insult the collective political conscience of the majority, and at best, they undermine democracy at the expense of autocratic rule. The Rule of Law become the

Rule of a Man, and freedom is relegated to oblivion. Africa should fight against this evil. Even with over economic advances, an OMS Rule will always lead to bondage, political disfranchisement and intolerance. Africa must resist OMS Rule. The African people must rise up and condemn OMS Rule, no matter the justification. Government by definitive tenure should be the gold-standard, and not life-presidency, no matter how great the leader should be.

20 TOOLS OF COLONIALISM: NAMES AND LANGUAGE

[Published: October 12th, 2020, *Lusaka Times, Muckrack*]

Let us put it in context. We say that we have achieved independence, but habits and practices don't lie. Let us start with the agents (tools) of Colonialism.

First, name change. When the colonists invaded Africa, they first changed African names, globalized African heritage and culturized African formations into Western authentics. Thus, for Zambia, for example, we least hear or write about Chuma who traversed the copious forests and provided guidance to Dr. David Livingstone. We hear more and write more about Livingstone. We dub him the discoverer of Mosi-oa-Tunya Falls, which he conveniently renamed Victoria Falls after an English Queen in the far West in England. I am called "Charles," a royalty name in England. Probably as I write this, a majority of Africans reading are named after Europeans. Their own heritage is forgotten.

Like in the USA where former slave masters still live in the psyche and mentals of their Black slave progenies, they still are remembered through their names which they had bequeathed through their names. In short, their legacy, which, apparently, was enslaving, degrading, humiliating, abusive and name it all, is preserved through names. It is the same in Africa. We are still called by their names. Surely, our parents wouldn't have pondered much on this, and naturally named us after former colonial enchanters. In future, shouldn't we be thinking of having more of "Chibesa Kundas", "Mwansa Malamas", "Mpezeni Ndhlovus", "Milupi Phiris," "Chavula Ngoyis," and etc.? Shouldn't we be thinking of renaming some of our streets, clubs, animals, forests, and, indeed, national monuments by our own unique African quadrisyllabics? Think about all that, and more.

Names, they submit to whoever calls on them, just don't forget that.

Second, language. The Bible gives us a clue: "And the LORD said, 'If they have begun to do this as one people speaking the same language, then nothing they devise will be beyond them. Come, let Us go down and confuse their language, so that they will not understand one another's speech.'"[32] Three things right there:

1. Language unifies;
2. Language breeds success
3. Language is a weapon of either enslavement or liberation.

Whose language you speak, that one you will always obey. It is just that simple. We may be proud of articulating foreign accents, but the glory is not, eventually, ours. It goes back to the one who owns it.

---

[32] Gen. 11:6-7

Those who conquered Africa, did it in four ways:

1. Language
2. Guns
3. Bible
4. Intrigue – call it machinations or diplomacy, it carries the same venom. They still do – we use their language (we have even gone to the extent of justifying its naturalization and nationalization); they have more in their arsenals (they are still producing weapons of mass destruction such as nuclear heads, but they wouldn't let us do the same), we have little to nothing; they are still preaching love, when our resources they milk with a globalized ferocity; and they are still measuring us by our bloating debt, their growing capital, and our cheap labor. It is the same old strategy, and it does not fail.

We still read them, about them, for them and with them. We read their books, quote their quotables and stock up our libraries with their "superior" acumens. Don't we? Books are not in our vocabulary, but one can conquer an empire, rob your inheritance and send you to an early grave, simply by a book. How many of you even know about my book, "Struggles of My People"? But you had ordered Dan Brown's, "Demons," even before it was released. You would have post-mailed, with long, passionate reviews in African newspapers the writings of European and American authors. This is while your own brilliant brains die in graves of illiteracy and neglect. We have idolized Shakespeare, memorialized Chaucer, invigorated Van Gore, and internalize Blake. While, at the same time, we have inferiorized our sages, bards, poets, thinkers and emerging writers. We don't purchase their works and we judge their mental stability and IQ to be base.

A second language, is just so, second. Everything you do with it will be second. Your best effort will remain second. Your greatest theories will continue to be second. Your best minds are second. Your greatest ingenuities, still second. And even your most eloquent orators, will just be second. So, why not capitalize on your first? Why not speak, write and think in Bemba, Nyanja, Lozi, Luvale, Tonga, and etc., and be first? No European or American power has ever, even remotely, contemplated making an African language first, though Mandarin, Cantonese, Spanish, French, they may. But here we are: We fill our schools with second-baked enchanters learning to think, believe, behave and act, second. Our problem, "We have many of these languages and dialects." And the next thing we do is we make it politics, and continue to be only second, even in politics itself.

Language conquers everything, just don't forget that.

21 TOOLS OF COLONIALISM: STANDARDS

[Published: October 23rd, 2020, *Lusaka Times, Muckrack*]

It is amazing that the elephant is always in the room, when it comes to pinning the real African issues. So, we gloat over everything in snippets of fear to offend, but how then can we heal the wounds of the past?

To advance my analogy to a wound, bandaging is only useful if the wound is first cleaned. But to cover a wound with all the virus or bacteria on it, is to encourage it to fester with horrible infections. And that is what we have done for Africa, when we fail to address real effects of Colonialism.

After slavery and Colonialism and since Neo-Colonialism, Africa and Africans have to measure up to Western standards. This includes culture, lifestyle, technology and even humanity, to select only four.

Let us begin with culture. When Europeans first came to Africa, they denigrated everything African. There was nothing "civilized" or "advanced" or "holy" in the practices and customs of Africa. A strong message was sent to Africans, "Don't worship your gods; they are idols," "Consider changing your birth, marriage and death customs to ours; yours are primitive," and so on. In the end, Africans began to pour scorn on their own ways of life and started to anchor for Westernism. In other words, anything that was not Western, was either evil, backward, unpolished or patently could not measure up to the authentic European standards. Western standards became African standard.

You think I am blubbing, how about today? How do Africans arrange their homes, conduct their marriages, bury their dead or even celebrate childbirth or childhood – it's all pegged upon how "we," in the West, do it.

We don't miss the West much, when we travel back to Africa; but I can't say the same the many years I have spent in the West. There is hardly nowhere I can go and authentically enjoy an African value theme. It comes in bits and pieces.

The story is different in Africa – from the billboards at the airports, to the media, to the news, to politics, in education, and with culture – it is as if I am back in Toronto all over again.

Why? Because Africa seems to have been made to forget its own value system. Somehow to be considered un-Western seems to be a bigger sin than to boldly declare, "Leave me alone, I want to sing, dance, talk, and dress-up like they do or did in Africa!"

Africa now seems to have no culture at all, and if it does, it is a modified form, tilting heavily towards Westernism.

Second, let us look at lifestyle. Somehow to look, feel or behave like a Westerner seems to be more authentic than being African-like. So, the clothes' labels, make-up type, and size and weight of the body are all to be standardized upon a White body or feel, or make or behavior. Thus, most of African women want to be "just a bit light", "less black", or "a little bit of straight hair" — without knowing, they have imbibed into Westernism. What about height – so, if one is shorter and a little bit fatter – you have crossed the line, you have not pegged to the stature of a true American standard for beauty or normalcy.

Does it mean that only those, who are lighter, taller and slimmer are truly humans and models, but life is not set that way. In fact, reality dictates otherwise – we find people loving people others would quirk at, "What did he see in her?" and vice-versa.

It is because the reality is different from the standards set by the media, Hollywood and fashion/beauty industry in the West. If our girl children do not display a Barbie-type body, does it mean that they are not beautiful enough?

It was not too long ago that Westerners came to Africa and insulted all the buttock-protruding women. To them, these African women were "ugly," and reason: Because they had big buts. Smaller people are somehow disparaged as "midgets" and bigger people are solidly criticized as, "fat."

So, now tell me, what is the ideal, and where did that come from? Not from Africa; it was perpetuated by Western conception of beauty and standard and anyone, anywhere, who did not measure up to "this" standard, was not, indeed, ideal or perfect.

"Oh, Africa, please, please, do not let anyone or anybody ever again infringe on, and impugn, your humanity. Africa should not strive to live by Western standards, unless those standards advance African culture, lifestyle, technology and humanity."

Colonialism – it robbed Africa of its own perfection. Kinky hair does not make an African ugly, and neither is her skin color or height or weight. Like everywhere else, "Beauty is in the eye of the beholder."[33] And the Dictionary is correct, "beauty cannot be judged objectively, for what one person finds beautiful or admirable may not appeal to another."

Oh, Africa, pretending to have Western beauty will not make you beautiful; you will always be second. Be just

---

[33] An English Proverb

who you are, of course, working within your own fascia to improve yourself.

Third, technology, and this may upset many and chaff others, yes, indeed, Africa had and continues to have, its own version of technology. Remember, if there is any race of people on earth (probably, with the exception of the Jews), Black Africans have survived extinction. Every calamitous event, such as slavery and Colonialism, were meant to wipe Africans out of the face of the earth.

How else can you explain the disregards, the mistreatments, the discriminations and ultimately, the killings of innocent Black Africans for over 400 years?

But Africa, and the Black people of Africa, have survived. They have done so, partly, because of technology, albeit, very simple technologies. This enabled them to cross ravaging rivers and dangerous lakes, manipulate dense and hazardous forests, tame wild and vicious animals, till arid and hostile lands and conquer natural disasters.

The Industrial Revolution and the Internet ages are not the only technology-shapers in history; though they are, and were, arguably, superior. But this does not mean that Africa did not have, and cannot have, authentic technologies.

Last, in this series, humanity. This was at the heart of both slavery and Colonialism, African-descended people were not humans at all. You see, modern rendition of this deals a dearth of justice to history; African people (especially Blacks) were considered less than property. Because, sometimes, one might have golden property and keep it in a safe, not Africans, they were up for abuse. They were not "cheap labor" they were "free, available, expendable, labor." They had no soul; they were only a conglomeration of flesh and sinews and tendons and bones and muscles. They were not human.

Let us tell the truth, it was mostly because they were deemed not to measure up to European or American standards of humanity. It is more onerous to be considered un-human than it is to be considered not a person.

In Canada, for example, until 1951, women were not considered persons, in the context of equality before the law. Another example: when Britain left Northern Rhodesia (Zambia) in 1964, those who were at the level of civil clerks became new leaders of the new nation.

To understand this, you have to consider the hierarchy that propelled the colonial machine. At the highest echelon was the Queen/King, then Minister responsible for colonies. Under him were Regional Commissioners, and below them District Commissioners/Governors. These then had a cortege of aristocratic bureaucracy running the day-to-day colonial machinery. Then you had the cadets and junior cadets. All these were Whites. A Black rank began at a clerk level, and even here, it was for the "most educated" African – who was probably a Standard Two.

To place this in a historical context, the battle to acquire human status for the Black Africans reached its height in 1919. In that year, the Covenant of the League of Nations was adopted. It was only here that considerations began to be had, as to whether Black Africans deserved the same human rights as their Western counterparts.

What they call "self-rule" is imbued in the idea that Africans were not human enough to rule themselves. The conception was related to how you can engage in mental and intellectual intercourse as to if a cat was left alone in the house without training it, could it survive the rigor of "doing things alone"?

Britain was reluctant to give independence to the Black Africans, somehow because Britain judged, "They cannot rule themselves." At the heart of this agenda was the idea that Black Africans were devoid of intellectual, and social, and let alone political competence to rule themselves.

There is no question that Britain had a Western-European standard of leadership, and by extension of humanity, in its mind. It was forgotten that Blacks had ruled themselves before Colonialism.

Neo-Colonialists, like Donald Trump, still refer to Africa and the African people as "shitholes." So, this humanity issue is not moot. Thankfully, countries, like Canada, have enacted legislation and policies, aimed at curbing this discriminatory injustice. *The Charter of Rights and Freedoms* is such a magnanimous Constitutional document in Canada.

As recent as October 20th, 2020, the Peel Regional Police, its board and the Ontario Human Rights Commission (OHRC) signed a memorandum of understanding (MOU) pledging to come up with and implement legally-binding measures to end systemic racism in policing.[34]

Blacks and their humanity are at the center of this understanding. This is one of the reasons I love Canada; its leaders have worked very hard to recognize Africa as an equal partner, not only in development, but in the recognition of Black Africans as humans. There is more to be done, though. Africa should not strive to live by Western standards, unless those standards advance African culture, lifestyle, technology and humanity.

---

[34] Shallima Maharaj, *Global News*

22 OBAMA: LONG WALK TO BLACK POWER

[Written between 2008 and 2010]

On a typical day, there would be three different channels showing in our apartment. Clarice would be watching one of the reality shows such as "So You Think You Can Dance, Canada" in the living room. Emmerance will be watching cartoons on Treehouse in her bedroom. And I would be watching news on CNN or soccer in my home office. But not on that Tuesday of November 4th, 2008. There was only one channel in the house, CNN. I knew it was to be a special day. Clarice has never been interested in politics. But on this Tuesday, she braved the whole night with me, comparing and analyzing the election results. At one time she said she wanted to doze-off but then said, "Wake me up when Florida is called." At that moment, I knew the results of the 2008 presidential elections in the United States would not only be historic but emotional.

From Selma to Montgomery

Martin Luther King, Jr. and James Bevel initiated the famous march from *Selma to Montgomery*. This march is considered an emotional and political peak of the American civil rights movement. The march was symbolic. It had to take three trials to finally succeed in reaching Montgomery. The first attempt resulted in the Bloody Sunday when over 600 marchers were attacked by state and local police on March 7th, 1965. The second march also flopped when police again attacked the marchers with billy-clubs and tear gasses. Only the third, and last, march successfully made it into Montgomery, Alabama. The route is memorialized as the *Selma to Montgomery National Voting Rights Trail*, a US National Historic Trail.

The history of the Black people has been one of trials and tribulations. *Selma to Montgomery* epitomizes that struggle. When they marched the first, second and third times on that trail, they were never discouraged. Although they suffered beatings and even imprisonments, they kept moving, with faith and hope only driving them. There is no race of a people on the face of this globe who have gone through the pain and shame of humanity like the Black race. From slavery to Colonialism to Apartheid and to racial discrimination, the

Black race has had the lion share of it. But like *Selma to Montgomery*, the Black spirit has proven resilient.

I have been to the Mountaintop

The history of African Americans is very similar in many respects with that of the deliverance of the Israelites from bondage in Egypt. The Israelites found themselves in bandage in Egypt after first trekking there as a privileged tribe under the prime ministerial mantle of Joseph. After the death of Joseph, a cruel Pharaoh who did not know Joseph feared that the Israelites would become too numerous in number and rise in revolt. So he enslaved them. But African Americans found themselves in the New World with the primary purpose of being slave labor.

After 430 years of heavy bondage, God sent the Israelites a savior in the name of Moses. Moses made speeches on behalf of the children of Israel and set them on their road to the Promised Land. Moses himself did not enter the Promised Land. However, God allowed him to see the land from the mountaintop:

> Then Moses went up from the plains of Moab to Mount Nebo, to the top of Pisgah, which is across from Jericho. And the LORD showed him all the land of Gilead as far as Dan…. Then the LORD said to him, 'This is the land of which I swore to give to Abraham, Isaac and Jacob, saying, I will give it to your descendants.' I have caused you to see it with your eyes, but you shall not cross over there.[35]

---

[35] Deuteronomy 34: 1-4

Moses' successor, Joshua, was to take the Israelites into the Promised Land. Joshua knew that he was not the savior, but only fulfilling the dream of Moses. It was Moses who had gone to the mountain to receive the instructions. It was Moses who had sacrificed his life for the deliverance of his people. But Joshua was important, too. He had to be prepared. He had to be courageous and decisive in order to bring the promise to fulfillment.

African Americans had their own Moses in Martin Luther King, Jr. A Baptist preacher and eloquent civil rights leader, King rose to the occasion and fought for equality and voting rights of the African Americans. Like Moses, he made historic speeches, and like Moses, he died before an African American could rise to power. But he had laid the foundation. On April 3rd, 1968 at Mason Temple, Church of God in Christ, in Memphis, Tennessee, he made the famous, "I Have Been to the Mountaintop" speech:

> Like anybody, I would like to live a long life. Longevity has its place. But I'm not concerned about that now. I just want to do God's will. And He's allowed me to go up to the mountain. And I've looked over. And I've seen the Promised Land. I may not get there with you. But I want you to know tonight, that we, as a people, will get to the Promised Land! And so I'm happy, tonight. I'm not worried about anything. I do not fear any man! Mine eyes have seen the glory of the coming of the Lord!!

King stated that he loved to live like anybody else. He wanted to see his children grow in his sight and to see the United States transcend race and judge people not by the color of their skins but by the content of their character. King saw death coming but he did not fear. He counted his own life as of no value compared to what it meant to his own people. He was willing to give up his own life for African Americans. Like Moses, he was not to enter into the Promised Land but only saw it from afar.

The Hands that Built America will Now Rule America

Solomon, the wisest man who ever lived, made the observation about four things that perturbed him: When a servant becomes president; when an unemployed person is filled with food; when a hateful woman is married; and finally when a maid succeeds her mistress.[36] He was correct. Like what Royson James wrote in the *Toronto Star*, "There will be a black man in the White House come January 20 and he won't be the janitor, the butler or a baker. Barak Obama will be running the joint as president of the United States of America…"

The beauty with such developments is that president-elect Obama will rule with a sense of justification on his side. But he will also rule with humility knowing that the blood of those who sacrificed for these victories await their own justification. There is no recorded history which has denied the reality that when a people suffer for a cause, and even die for it, and they fail to win in the end. From the blood of the martyrs who die for religious causes to the blood of freedom fighters who die for political causes to the blood of philanthropies who die for the ordinary people, resounds the genial truth that payday will always come.

---

[36] Proverbs 30: 21-23

Unorthodox Means of Victory

When history has been made, it has most of the time been made by the most unlikely of humanity. It is human nature to expect victory to come from the most skilled, power from the most educated and fame from the most privileged. But Solomon chose to differ:

> I returned and saw under the sun that – the race is not to the swift, nor the battle to the strong, nor bread to the wise, nor riches to men of understanding, nor favor to men of skill; but chance and time happen to them all.[37]

When Joseph's brother sold him to the merchants, they thought that it would be the end of Joseph. But divine providence had other plans. Joseph was destined to be Egypt's most successful prime minister. But what is amazing is the way an Israelite would find himself or herself in Egypt. By all accounts it was impossible for an Israelite to be in a position of authority there, and let alone a prime minister. Nevertheless, even a potential president will not be suspect when he is shipped as a slave. It happened to Joseph, to Moses, to Obama's ancestors and is bound to happen again. Peter correctly put it, "The stone which the builders rejected has become the chief cornerstone."[38]

Lesson for Zambia's Electoral Process

The Americans teach us so many lessons. But one of the most important lessons they teach us is how to man

---

[37] Ecclesiastes 9:11
[38] 1 Peter 2: 7

an electoral process. Imagine if the United States was Zambia and electing the first Black president in history? It is likely that history would not have been made. There is a serious problem with our electoral process. The system in many instances does not reflect the will of the people. This happens in spite of the fact that our election results are based on a simple majority. The US system is hooked on an Electoral College which chooses a president based on the electoral votes allocated to each state. This means that the president-elect may not be the candidate with the popular vote, the case of Bush and Al Gore in 2000, for instance. Of course, the 2008 elections were different where president-elect Obama won both the Electoral College and the popular vote.

Even with our simple system, we still fail to inject credibility in our electoral process in Zambia. Under such a system as ours, an incumbent could always easily manipulate the votes in his or her favor. The will of the people is rejected, and a popular candidate may not win the elections. Coupled with this is the fact that the Electoral Commission of Zambia which has been mandated with the duty to regulate elections in Zambia is not autonomous in reality. On paper, yes, it is. But where the president can influence who sits on the commission as its chairman undermines the fairness and transparency of the electoral system.

As we watch the United States making history and in the same vein breaking from its past of racial discrimination and xenophobia, we should be asking ourselves very serious questions. Are we going to determine to change the way we conduct elections in Zambia? Are we going to remain in the shambles of dishonesty, power-hungry politicization and election-result theft? If we are going to progress from putting mediocre and imprudent presidents in our State House, we must endeavour to fight to change our electoral process in Zambia.

Benedictions

Obama may have inherited insurmountable economic and military problems in the US, but history has been made. To God be the glory, that once again we Black people can walk with heads high knowing that there is no challenge on the face of the earth we cannot master. We are a people on a mission, a mission to build positive legacies for the whole world to emulate. Congratulations Obama, and may God give you wisdom and courage to rule the greatest nation on earth.

23 BARACK OBAMA: TRIUMPH OVER CYNICISM

[Written in June 2008]

During one of his campaign interviews Senator Barack Obama was asked by a journalist why African-Americans were afraid that he was running for the highest office in the United States of America. Pausing for few seconds, Senator Obama answered something to the effect that, African-Americans ought to be healed from a culture of fear of failure.

For us who have devoted most of our time to seeking for a just society, this is an historic event. If a woman becomes a president of a developed nation, that is very important news. If a woman should become the president of the United States of America, that is revolutionary. But if a Black-American becomes a presidential nominee of one of the two major United States political parties, history is made. Barack Obama has entered into the annals of the greatest and the mightiest, the bravest and the fearless who closed their ears to the voices of fear and prejudice and forged ahead to claim an historic trophy.

Senator Obama's victory is the victory for the whole world. In the Thursday, June 5th, 2008, edition of the *24 Hours Magazine* in Toronto, a hairdresser is quoted as having said in Mexico City, "Obama is of the people."

And she could not be very far from the truth. American presidency has been dominated by White males for as long as the United States was founded. African-Americans have made important strides in all fields, but the clinching of the nomination of Senator Obama is second to none. This event will change the way people look at racial discrimination forever, no matter who wins the presidency. America has become of age; the world has been healed.

On Tuesday, June 3rd, 2008, I followed the final results of the presidential primaries in the US for the most part of the day. Around 10 pm Senator Obama gave a speech in St. Paul, Louisiana where Martin Luther King, Jr. made the "I Have Dream" in the sixties. Obama's speech, "It's Our Time" is the answer to, "I Have a Dream" speech. In his graves, King should have raved; his dream has been realized through Barack Obama.

As an African living in America (Canada) I see this event as a culmination of all that has gone before, the sacrifices, pains, and endurance of the people of color in America. They sacrificed their dignity, pride and blood for a time such as this. Now the way we see other people will permanently change. Character and not color will define how we relate to one another. Obama's triumph is the triumph over racism, racial discrimination, and prejudice. It is a triumph not only for the American people, but for the entire world as well. Long live Obama, long live the nation of goodwill, love and equality.

24 END OF RULE BY POLITICIANS – DID BORIS JOHNSON DUPE THE QUEEN?

[Published: September 24th, 2019, *Lusaka Times*]

Immediately after the decision was released by the UK Supreme Court (UKSC) on September 24th, 2019, the majority who commented said, "Nobody expected this…" Some shouted, "It's unbelievable, shocking…." The reactions themselves, rather than the unanimous ruling of all eleven Supreme Court judges, handed down by Lady Brenda Hale, is what seems to be shocking to many. But in reality, both the nature of the decision and the tremor it has generated, should be shocking to all. These are my reasons.

1. Because Politicians have, hitherto, Circumvented the Law

Until this decision, it had become fashionable for

Parliament to be used just as a rubber-stamp for the whims of the politicians in power. This did not matter whether that Parliament was found in a nation with Parliamentary Democracy (such as the UK, Canada, and etc.) or in a Presidential Democracy (such as the USA, Zambia, and etc.). It was that ardent campaigner and businesswoman's sentiments that solidified this notion: "It was very nervous up to the moment…there was little guarantee that we would win this."[39] This should shock every democracy lover and Rule of Law agitator. The people had given up on the power of courts or the law to rule. The world had resigned itself to the caprice of politicians to manipulate the law and "abuse" Parliament for its own hidden agendas. That's why people were surprised at the decision.

2. Because Abuses of Power have, hitherto, been Cloaked in Divided Court Decisions

We all know that ruling parties, presidents and Prime Ministers, have been abusing power and running away with it. This has been possible because the auras of people-power have been diminished. In Parliamentary systems, prorogation of Parliament, or in presidential systems, use of executive emergency orders, have all meant that the will of the people have been secondary. And to add salt to injury, courts had been, hitherto, justifying-chambers of the abuses of the politicians. It's no wonder everyone did not expect the unanimous decision of the UKSC. Faith in the judiciary all over the world have been slowly eroding because there has been very little distinction between political quirks and judicial

---

[39] Gina Miller

activism. Each time a court rendered a divided decision on a matter that, in the judgment of society, ought to have been unanimous, it made politicians bold. Because, when they partially lost in court, they still argued that some judges stood with them in their abuses of office and authority. That's why this decision is, ironically, landmark, because it refuses to side with the abuse of power, it decides to stand up for principle, the Rule of Law, and fundamentals of good governance. The decision says, "No-judge agrees with Boris Johnson, in part on or whole." If there was even a single judge who dissented, Boris Johnson would stand on the world platform and declare that he had at least one ally in the UKSC. That's how politicians have spun their undemocratic tendencies into placards of lame victory. But as far as the UKSC is concerned, the Prime Minister broke the law, and his decision to prorogue Parliament is as if it never even happened.

3. Because Even the Queen could be Misled

Politicians mislead everybody, in the case of Boris Johnson, including the Queen of England. The UKSC ruled that the decision to advise the Queen to prorogue Parliament was unlawful. The Queen had earlier consented to the prorogation of Parliament. This is very informing – it means that, hitherto, even venerated offices such as that of the Queen of England, had been subservient to the whims of the ruling politicians. Indeed, we know that the regal bureau is only ceremonial. However, this, effectively, means that democracy had fallen prey to the Tyranny of the Majority and the inviolable power of one-man.

In conclusion, the world has a reason to celebrate this landmark, unanimous UK decision. This is because it's a UK decision, the birther of the *Magna Carta*, and the land that bequeathed to Western political and legal cultures, their legal and political systems. At least in the interim, this decision curbs on political extremities of those who rule nations as if they have been given a license to abuse power and privileges.

25 ARE EVANGELICALS GAINING THE WORLD AND LOSING THEIR OWN SOULS?

[Published: January 28th, 2018, *Lusaka Times*]

We are living in interesting times. We are witnessing moral erosion in governments. But no-one anticipated that Evangelical leaders would steep so low as to justify infidelity in the guise of political policy or material acquisition. I will lay parity to three issues: Rising moral turpitude in the Age of Trump; Evangelical secularism; and corruption unrestrained.

Rising Moral Turpitude in the Age of Trump

In any epoch, where great privilege is given, great responsibility is demanded. In the old ages, Babylon, Greece, Rome, British and now American empires, those who conquered the world also had a great responsibility to influence behavior. But even at its vilest echelon, leaders of empires and mighty nations knew that their example was necessary to the sanity, stability and vitality of their nations.

Powerful leaders, such as presidents of the United States, do not just say, do or react to things. Whatever they say, do or decide has, directly or indirectly, impact on their people and the world at large. In the past, America has prided in electing men who, admittedly have been weak, but who were expected (in fact) to display great moral stamina in the governance of their people's affairs. They were expected to stand on principles, respect the Rule of Law and lead their people with unquestionable integrity. Trump is eroding all these, slowly and surely. The American president has failed to stand on principles, is brutalizing press freedom, cannot admit to his own moral foibles, has uttered degrading and racist statements against minority groups, women and immigrants, and has taken advantage of a materialistic evangelical Church in America. For sure, this may fulfill some political point, but in the end, the world is at risk of demagoguism and lost moral vivacity.

Evangelical Secularism

Jesus said that the love of money, not money itself, is the root of all evil. Wasn't he right? Generally, the Evangelical Church is becoming more secular and devoid of moral gravitas than in any age. The working mantra in many an Evangelical Church is hypocrisy. It is deficient in strong leaders who cannot be tossed to and from by the wild winds of enticements. All these leaders are preoccupied with is "money": Money for this, money for the kingdom, money for material "blessings." They are willing to support politicians who promise them free money or who will "align their policy according to the Bible." This last issue is very deceptive. A politician ought only to recite, "The Lord's Prayer" or declare he is anti-abortion or anti-same-sex marriage, and these leaders will be bought. The result is that they will shut their eyes to the moral short-comings of the politician and accept all of his incendiary and tribal politics as truth. They will justify his election as the will of God (but they will not accept all those previous presidents and politicians before him as God's choices, too).

Corruption Unrestrained

The marriage of the first two points will only strengthen corruption, especially in economically struggling and politically undemocratic nations. Why, because America (in its own weaknesses) is generally seen as a moral leader in the world. With its being weak on morality under Trump, authoritarians all over the world will justify their own behaviors. They will abuse the law, discard principles, undermine justice, erode morality and engage in corrupt practices. They will not fear reprisal, because the United States are themselves under siege. Why again, because the Christian voice which has sanitized morality and provided fidelity to politics is wanting. Church leaders are more interested in "making money" than in Christ-like leadership. Some Church leaders are lukewarm, complicity, unforgiving (unless the forgiveness will create them opportunities with political echelons), and in the name of God, are stealing their congregants' wealth and savings.

I posit that the worst culprit of this moral erosion and corruption will be Africa. The West, and to some extent, South-East Asia, may be able to weather this moral tsunami. The West will manage Trumpism, because they have strong institutions and growing free voice, but Africa may not.

26 AFROPOSITIVE

[Written between 2005 and June 2007]

This July 1st, 2007, Canada will be 140 years old. This Canadian birthday is special; there is a birth of a new era, a new dimension of racial equalization. It is the appointment of Michaelle Jean as Governor General. The Governor General (GG) is a ceremonial Head of State while the Prime Minister is only Head of Government. In short, Canada is led by a Black woman. This is huge. It is a mammoth achievement for Canada, and Africa, too. Her Excellency, the Right Honorable Michaelle Jean is already changing things. Of particular interest to me is the idea of being Afropositive. She explains this idea in this way:

> We look at Africa as hopeless: People begging, misery, illness everywhere-a lost continent. That's not Africa; it's also about hope. Through indifference, people feel powerless, fatalistic. This is something I can't stand.

Yes, that's what Africa has not been able to stand. The way Africa is portrayed leaves a lot to be desired. Africa is indeed about hope, and the people, too. Being Afropositive is about representing Africa equitably and with the dignity it deserves. It is about telling the truth – the truth that there is hope and progress in Africa. The truth is Africa is also about technology, democracy and development. A Black woman as GG means the defeat of racism and racial discrimination. Racism and hatred only destroy our beautiful planet.

The hallmark of hatred lies in its ability to manipulate truth. Its strength is in prejudice. Nations have fought and society has been broken asunder due to preconceived ideas about race. Some people have hated others of a different race simply because they have distorted truth. Some races erroneously believe they are superior to others. Things are changing, not only in Canada and Africa, but all over the world. My dream is to see a world ridden of all forms of discrimination. A world in which we can all be players on an equal footing. A world in which we are all valued for who we are, not because of our history.

27 PREACHING AND THE COVID-19 PANDEMIC

[Published: May 2020, Facebook.com/charlesmwewa]

The Covid-19 outbreak is not the end of the world; it's one of the signs of the beginning of the end. Consider Matthew 24: 7-8: "For nation will rise against nation, and kingdom against kingdom. And there will be famines, *pestilences*, and earthquakes in various places. All these are the beginning of birth pains." Covid-19 ("pestilences") is just like earthquakes or famine or wars. When we see these things, we don't say that it's the end; they depict the beginning of the end. Consider a woman who is pregnant and about to give birth. The cervical effacement (thinning) and dilation (opening) must be 100 percent effaced and 10 cm dilated before a vaginal delivery. This is because during the first stage of labor, the cervix opens and thins out to allow the baby to move into the birth canal. In scatological terms, "pestilences" are like the first stages of vaginal labor. We could say a woman is 2 cm dilated. According to the Bible, the last sign of the end is the Gospel spreading. This is like the 10 cm dilation: "And this Gospel of the kingdom will be preached in the whole world as a testimony to all nations, and then the end will come."[40]

The Covid-19 outbreak is not the subtle way of introducing the Mark of the Beast ("666"). The Mark of the Beast (MOB) is not a disease; it's the number of a Man, a leader: "This calls for wisdom. Let the person who has insight calculate the number of the beast, for it is the number of a man. That number is 666."[41] Note that this calls for "wisdom" and interpretation. Unwise or less detailed or the ignorant will not decipher this. Review of the Bible shows that MOB will be revealed during the "Seventh Trumpet [Third and Last Woe]", and this is far away before the "Seven Angels with Seven Plagues"[42] have been released. The Anti-Christ and MOB will be a Man who will emerge probably from Union of Nations in Europe, and subsequently claim his throne in Jerusalem ("Abomination that Causes Desolation: "So when you see standing in the holy place 'the abomination of desolation,' described by the prophet Daniel (let the reader understand)."[43] At that time, he will unify the economic transaction system and exalt the chip technology.

---

[40] Matthew 24:14
[41] Rev. 13:18
[42] Rev. 15:1 ff
[43] Matthew 24:15

Preach that Christians should not fear the pandemic but they should not be ignorant of how it spreads and that they should take precautions. Telling people to continue their lives as usual without taking precautions like self-isolation, social distancing or staying at home, is like tempting God. God only protects you if you don't know that what you are drinking is poison or if you are going through persecution: "They shall take up serpents; and if they drink any deadly thing, it shall not hurt them; they shall lay hands on the sick, and they shall recover."[44]

Note here that when you are inadvertently bitten by a snake or you mistakenly drink poison, or you get infected by the Covid-19 even after taking all the precautions, you can have people pray for you to be healed. Similarly, if God has provided you with smart physicians, experts and scientists, that is His will to inform you so that you don't die because of ignorance: "…my people are destroyed from lack of knowledge."[45]

Lack of knowledge will kill you, so will be willful blindness to the spread of Covid-19. The pastor's job during the Covid-19 pandemic is to warn and educate their congregation to know about the Covid-19, take precaution, avoid crowding (do social distance, isolation and etc.). It is not faith to know the dangers of the disease and still subject yourself to its venom; such people will surely die.

Preaching in Church buildings is not necessary; it is a convenience. Jesus Himself educated and advised: "You worship what you do not know; we worship what we do know, for salvation is from the Jews. But a time is coming and has now come when the true worshipers will worship

---

[44] Mark 16:18
[45] Hosea 4:6

the Father in spirit and in truth, for the Father is seeking such as these to worship Him. God is Spirit, and His worshipers must worship Him in spirit and in truth."[46]

The building is not a designated place of worship under New Testament guidelines; it's a place of convenience. However, during a pandemic like Covid-19, a Church building or physical meeting becomes an inconvenience and even dangerous. God will still be there when you remotely "gather or assemble", "…because where two or three have come together in my name, I am there among them."[47]

The Bible was written before the introduction of social media, cellphones, TV, and so on. Now we know that with these advanced forms of technology, we can "gather" remotely and achieve the same purpose gathering physically achieves. Therefore, and in these Covid-19 times, it is wiser and better not to meet physically in Church; utilize all forms of technology out there. If you preach that it is "holy" and "obedience" and "faith" to gather physically when you know it is not bad, it is not only unwise, but also sin: "If anyone, then, knows the good they ought to do and doesn't do it, it is sin for them."[48]

The primary, unsaid, reason why most pastors are afraid of Covid-19 and the need for social distancing and so on, is not spiritual, it is financial. This is not an unreasonable fear; most Churches depend on tithes and offerings from those who frequent and attend their physical congregations. Covid-19 and the requirement to social distance, may not only portend danger but may also take away the only means of survival most Church

---

[46] John 4:22-24
[47] Matthew 18:20
[48] James 4:17

leaders know. So, it is a big challenge. I think that when measures for social distancing, and especially the proscription of more than 50 people to gather are prescribed, Ministers of Gospel and similarly-situated professionals should be taken into account. It is wrong, for example, to proscribe more-than-50 gatherings and then not to provide an economic survive kit to such affected professionals. How then will they feed their families, pay bills, and basically live? In this case, the cure will be more deadly than the pandemic.

There must be both political will and common-sensical idealization required for Church leaders to survive the pandemic financially. The following are just suggestions:

(a) Adopt online Church or via social media or phone.

(b) Ask members to continue giving offerings via email Interac, direct deposit, or whatever paid system of money transfer available locally or internationally.

(c) Access government stimulus/rescue money to pay workers (payroll), rent and run other services, if your government has the capacity.

(d) Large Churches with bigger/fat banking savings now give back to the small local Churches if those local Churches cannot meet their budgets because of maximum 50 people required for gatherings.

(e) Trust God for uncommon and unusual ways of delivering your food and money for needs, consider, "You will drink from the brook, and I have directed the ravens to supply you with food there."[49]

(f) Pray, and God can do far more than you can ask or imagine, consider, "Now to him who is able to do immeasurably more than all we ask or imagine, according to his power that is at work within us..."[50]

(g) Be creative and ask from charities, NGOs or foundations set up for such needful times, consider, "Ask and it will be given to you; seek and you will find; knock and the door will be opened to you."[51]

(h) But don't crook people, lie to people or use people or expose them to Covid-19 without disclosing the real motive for such risky maneuverings.

(i) Don't disobey the law put in place by your government. When you disobey and you suffer, don't say that God is allowing you to be through persecution. It is just an unwise approach and is not sanctioned by God, consider, "Everyone must submit himself to the governing authorities (the 'law'), for there is no authority except that which is from God. The authorities that exist have been appointed by God. Consequently, the one who resists authority is opposing what God has set in place, and those who do so will bring judgment on themselves."[52]

(j) As a Minister, don't succumb to temptations, do good always, "...if you suffer for doing what is right,

---

[49] 1 Kings 17:4
[50] Ephesians 3:20
[51] Matthew 7:7
[52] Romans 13:1-2

God will reward you for it..."[53]

Tailor your message and preach in context, towards a unifying, knowledge-based and Christ-glorifying message. It is not the role of the Ministers of Gospel (pastors, and etc.) to pay people money or create jobs for people; that is the reasons governments are elected to do. The clergy's job is summarized in the following: "...to equip the saints for works of ministry, to build up the body of Christ, until we all reach unity in the faith and in the knowledge of the Son of God, as we mature to the full measure of the stature of Christ..."[54] It is a two-fold objective with three transcendental outcomes (unifying, knowledge-based and Christ-glorifying message):

(a) To equip the body – or to prepare, teach, school the members in the relevant doctrine. This also includes taking the available guidelines from government and encouraging the members to follow them. Teach them to obey the law and keep away from sin (remember, sin is the transgression of the law); and

(b) To build-up or encourage – the Covid-19 period is the ultimate moment to encourage the members. Most people are discouraged, afraid and hopeless. Your job is to lift up their spirit, encourage them to obey the law (and not to disregard it) and to give them direction when they seem lost. And, of course, to cerebrate death and provide last prayers, if some succumb to the virus.

---

[53] 1 Peter 3:14
[54] Ephesians 4:12-13

Ministers of the Gospel should stay close to achieving these goals during their Covid-19 period ministration.

28 NOT THE TIME TO OPEN CHURCHES

[Published: April 26th, 2020, *Zambian Eye*]

There are rumors the Zambian president has directed that Churches open in the midst of the coronavirus pandemic. State House (Zambian Government House) has, however, "clarif[ied] that His Excellency, Dr. Edgar Changwa Lungu, President of the

Republic of Zambia, has not directed Churches to open. In his address to the nation on Friday, the President said; 'I have decided that some activities such as the following may continue being undertaken normally subject to adhering to public health regulations, guidelines and certification…"

Africa, Zambia, included, is, of all continents, the least prepared and the least-resourced to fight the coronavirus (Covid-19). Zambia is not capable of fighting the pandemic. There are not enough, equipped hospitals. There are less well-trained specialized physicians. There is no SafetyNet to provide healthcare and treatment. And there are not enough Personal Protective Equipment (PPE) and ventilators to aid in the combat against Covid-19, should it invade Zambia full throttle. The best remedy to Covid-19 in Zambia is prevention. Nothing more.

Through social distancing, closure of worship centers, closure of contact businesses and sports and any such similarly-situated activities, the nation will be better placed than otherwise to defeat the pandemic. The disease has not reached its apex in Zambia – and this is the best time to take all necessary precautions to limit its spread. Coronavirus is already in Zambia, and that is the danger of it. That once it comes, it can only be stopped by either people not coming in contact or by people knowing their statuses so that they can either self-isolate or be quarantined. A Church, a congregation, provides contact or proximal association for people. It is by design a breeding ground for the spread of Covid-19. It does not take revelation or rocket science to know this. And the Government of Zambia knows this very well. To make matters worse, Zambian Churches may not have enough masks, available water sources and enough sanitary disinfectants to brace against the communalism of more than fifty persons in one place.

The president may be ill-advised, or even threatened by some religious figures that God would not allow His people to be infected because of Bible injunctions that inform on drinking poison and not dying. Such would be misinterpretation and misunderstanding of Scriptures. The president could, similarly, have been influenced by political or religious figures in Zambia who depend on the goodwill and the congregation of the people to collect offerings, which due to Covid-19 restrictions, may be running out. Such reasoning may be reasonable, but is inimical to the wellbeing and good health of the people. The danger of leaving Churches open is that it will expose widely the entire nation to Covid-19, not only to those who will be congregating. People in those meetings will infect each other and then take the infection further to other people they will interact with in mini-buses, marketplaces and homes.

The Zambian government should act boldly, resolutely and decisively and stop all Church meetings of a certain number. But it should also provide short-term financial relief to pastors and priests in full-time employment. Pastors and priests should also act wisely and creatively and invent smart ways of continuing preaching and collecting some money from their congregation. But there is a caveat: Don't collect money from people who have no financial sources of income during the Covid-19 pandemic. Some Churches should consider meeting the payroll needs of some of their smaller branches through the saving reserves they have amassed in good, non-Covid-19 pandemic times.

No government should foolishly subject its people to the pandemic. No Church leader should demand physical meetings during this time. Prayer for the pandemic to end should continue in homes and online. Covid-19 shall surely end, with God's intervention as well as through the intelligence of science. But until then, Church building-gatherings should remain closed to the public.

29 PRESIDENTIAL LEADERSHIP IN PANDEMIC TIMES

[Written during the Covid-19 Pandemic]

The quality of leadership for presidents is critical in crisis times, and no times are as critical as these Covid-19 outbreak times. There are three qualities that must be harnessed during the global pandemic period for presidential leadership:

Judgment;
National coordination/mobilization/cooperation;
And responsible use of emergency powers.

Judgment

(a) Ability to collect data and process information
(b) Ability to appoint the right mangers
(c) Prescience – ability to read the graphs and anticipate changes
(d) Decisive, quick and calculated decision-making

National Coordination (Mobilization/cooperation)

(a) Prompt coordination with provinces/states
(b) Resource mobilization and distribution
(c) Reporter-in-chief: daily and impactful national briefs
(d) Swift political coordination and economic legislation

Responsible Use of Emergency Powers

(a) Restrict movements
(b) Mete out sanctions
(c) Monitor progress – these powers should not last for long

30 POST-COVID-19 AFRICAN ERA

[Written during the Covid-19 Pandemic, Original/Unmodified]

> "As long as poverty, injustice, and gross inequality persist in our world, none of us can truly rest."
> - Nelson Mandela

Introduction

Many minds have attempted to understand why despite all efforts, Black people of Africa, and Black Americans in the USA, Blacks in Canada, Europe or anywhere they may be found, have struggled to survive economically and otherwise. Some have ruminated over issues such as color of the skin. Implicit in this ideation is the thinking that there is something wrong with being Black. Some have advanced identity, critical racial theorems as such as Black people have generally lower mental IQs; or political conspiracy theories like Black people are not capable of leadership or of governing themselves; or economic mantras like Blacks are incapable of managing money. In the light of the global protests taking place against police terrorism and racial injustice, I would like to provide a concise but tethered resume of what I believe to be the root cause of Black mistreatment, poverty and injustice. Inequalities and lack of equity, and not color, are the foundations that foster racism. I will then end with what I believe to be the future of Africa in the post-Covid-19 world. I want to disclaim from the outset that this article does not claim that all Whites are racists. However, everyone who harbors inequality sentiments is included.

It's not all about color; it has everything to do with a history of inequalities.

First, I wish to state, in no uncertain terms, that Blacks are not less than Whites in any way, form or shape. I wish, further, to dispute the idealism that color is Black people's liability. To the contrary, color has nothing to do with the brutal mistreatment Blacks have, historically, suffered at the hands of non-Blacks. Color or racism has been the tool (the means, rather than the end) that non-Blacks have used to malign and unjustly disparage Blacks, whether this has happened in North America, Europe, Asia, South America, the Pacific, or sadly, right on the African continent.

Second, the real reason why Blacks have been treated unfairly, poorly, unjustly, discriminatorily, and even murdered and imprisoned disproportionately, is rooted, generally, in the history of the Black people, and specifically, the White people's fear of being equal with Blacks. It has nothing to do with color, genetics or Black incompetence. Blacks have built civilizations, Western infrastructure, and have succeeded in whichever endeavour they have engaged in where rules have been fair to all. The White's historical fear to be equal with Blacks has been dangerously entrenched into the psyche that it has become a system. It is a system and, sadly, it works. Therefore, it has been perpetuated in just about every discipline: Governments, education and academia, media, military, trade and commerce, sports, social relations, politics, law and justice, law-enforcement, international organizations and religion, to mention only a few. In fact, when on July 4th, 1776, the thirteen United

States in America assembled in Congress, they unanimously identified the bug in their midst (inequality) and made a declaration: "We hold these truths to be self-evident, that all men are created equal, that they are endowed by their Creator with certain unalienable Rights, that among these are *life, liberty* and the pursuit of *happiness.*"[55] The moment the world begins to believe that all peoples are, in fact, equal, that will be the moment racial injustices will begin to fade.

Third, to use the most contemporary illustration, racism is used as a weapon to prevent Blacks from being equal to their White counterparts. Consider the presidencies of Barack Obama (Black) and Donald Trump (White). It does not take rocket science to note that Trump cannot compare to the leadership prowess that Obama displayed as president of a democratic state. However, because of the historical inequalities imbedded in the psyche of some White Americans, Trump, and similarly-situated Whites, are mortally injured to contemplate that a Blackman was more capable of democratic leadership than Trump was. The result is in the behavior Trump and his supporters displayed: Reversing every good Obama did; advancing an unfounded Obamagate conspiracy theory; and campaigning to disqualify Obama from being a USA citizen. At the root of this hatred and angst is the fear of being equal.

Fourth, Blacks, too, are indirectly complicit in their being treated unequally. And this lies, consequentially, in historical injustices of slavery and Colonialism. In West Africa where America bought most slaves, African chiefs sold what was valuable to them. Americans bought what

---

[55] Emphasis added

was equally valuable to them, but for a different purpose. The able-bodied young men and "fertile" girls that Black chiefs traded for pieces of mirror glass and ornaments, left Africa to ingloriously cultivate the plantations and haciendas of their White masters. Africa lost viable human and capital resources in human terms; America and Europe gained in terms of free, expendable labor force. In both cases, Blacks lost.

Those who were sold were put to slavery usage, deprived of humanity and reduced to mere property. The Africa the slavers left was sickly, old and unable to develop itself and perpetually depending on the same slavers and captors to provide handouts to them. In trading able-bodied, energetic Blacks and then only put them to below human-standard use, was a clear signal and sign that Whites regarded Blacks as unequals.

People are slowly realizing the interlinkage between modern injustices to historical slavery. For example, the recent tearing down of Edward Colston, a 17th century merchant slave trader and throwing it into a river, in Britain, and the toppling of Confederate General Williams Carter Wickham, in USA, allude to that fact. And, of course, one needs not go far but review the entrenchment of the conception of unequalness in the minds of some White Americans by considering the comparison *Fox News* made on June 5th, 2020. *Fox News* compared how the markets rose at the murder of Martin Luther King Jr. in 1968, and among others, the unceremonial and brutal killing of George Floyd by a White police officer in Minneapolis on May 25th, 2020. According to *Fox News* (which it later apologized for); the markets cerebrate the racial killings of Black Americans.

Although Fox News, apologized, however, they simply stated the obvious. Out of 500, 500 Fortune

CEOs in USA, there are only four (4) Black Americans. And yet Black Americans spent around $1.4 trillion in USA in 2019. In a layperson's language, Black Americans are still powering the economy of the USA without enjoying or owning its machines.

In Africa today, Western (mostly White owned) corporations own economic stays of most countries. And this also has its genesis in Colonialism. While the White colonial masters physically left Africa, they have returned in terms of business and trade. They still own Africa's means of production. Just like the African descendants sold the valuable able-bodied men and women to White Europe and America, their Black offspring now still sell their most precious mines, minerals, land and human capital to the West and Europe. And these have been cleverly embroiled in such terms and practices as "American Experience," whereby new immigrants from Africa are subjected to menial and base jobs even though they may come to the West with degrees and vital experiences.

It is not uncommon to find an African graduated lawyer or medical doctor driving a taxi – because his education is shunned and all he or she has invested in his life is only equal to a low job fit for an uneducated White American or European.

This injustice does not happen in Africa. For the most part, less educated Whites still get prestigious jobs in Africa. The problem is not racial; the problem is fundamentally equality. Some White Americans or Europeans cannot stand the fact that Black people can be equal with them. And this has permeated institutions and do form the mental framework of policy-makers and political leaders. It is the same thinking and experience in every sector of Western society – disproportional number of incarcerations. For example, although Blacks made up around 8.3% of the population in Toronto in 2012, about 86% of prisons constituted Black prisoners. The Toronto police had introduced a carding system in which they had increased their monthly revenues by targeting Blacks on the road to dish out traffic tickets, criminal citations and charges. Although this system was stopped, it was not without protests and sacrifices made by Black people and Black lawyers, most of whom became victims of the system; some lost their licenses to practice law, others died very sad deaths.

There is also a misconception that equipping and training police will result in good policing. To the contrary. Most police departments are well trained and equipped in Western formations. However, because of the culture and history of inequalities, the police have continued to abuse the people's human rights and fundamental dignity. What is required is equalizing the provision of services in communities of color. Most White dominated police departments erroneously believe that Black-dominated areas are harbingers of criminal activities, and they may have a point. But all this point to the unequal distribution of wealth, power and services to Black communities.

Most Blacks are found in communities with poor infrastructure, poor schools and poor healthcare, just as their forefathers and mothers experienced during and after slavery. Equality is the answer. Some of the resources spent on police should be channeled to the people in communities of color, to improve their lives.

White slave owners in the Americas totally destroyed the future of Black Americans. They owned them as property. They destroyed their conception of family – children born to slaves were also slaves. They denied the

Blacks of earnings, even if the Blacks worked hard and long hours with broken bones and slashed backs. This was the beginning of poverty among Black Americans. Even after slavery was abolished, Blacks did not have the assets to compete favorably in the new economic environment they found themselves. As slaves, they had no education. In fact, it was a crime for a Black slave to be found or seen pursuing an education. The best way to keep inequalities advancing is to deny one of an education. Education has the propensity to liberating the mind and action the soul. This was denied to Black people. Even when slavery had long ended, segregation in education in USA propagated the same denial of education. Poor education is the same as no education at all.

The same attitude was perpetuated in colonial Africa. Africans were not given any priorities when it came to education. When most African countries became independent in the early 1960s, they had very few "educated" people. In Zambia, for example, those who inherited government were clerks in the colonial regime. Suddenly they were given the reigns of "power." With scant education and zero experience, what were they supposed to do? At independence in Zambia in 1964, there were 100 or less college or university graduates, against a population of about three and half million people. As a consequence of this lack of education and experience, the first African leaders resorted to the very masters who had abused them for expertise and trade connections. In short, the Africans achieved political independence, but remained apron-tied to their colonial masters. By 1980s, the former White colonial masters had effectively returned as owners of African means of production. By the 1990s, corporate Africa was in the hands of, mostly White-headed, International Monetary Fund (IMF), the World Bank and Western, mostly White-owned, investors. In other words, the wealth of Africa was again not in the hands of Africans, but of the White corporate giants. Africans had to borrow what was inherently theirs. They, sadly, continue to do so today, where Africa only "owns" the land, and nothing else.

One has just to see the video of George Floyd being squeezed off his life in broad-day light. The cavalier manner in which Derek Chauvin (White police officer) murdered George Floyd is a testament to this postulation. Such mind-off killing is only reminiscent of a person killing say, a chicken, or something that has no equal human value. If one was seen killing an animal like that, that person would face the wrath of animal-lovers and activists. And George Floyd is just among many who have been killed without regard to dignity or humanity. In the mind of Derek Chauvin, George Floyd was not equal to him, and therefore, he deserved to be killed in a manner worse than a rabid dog.

Fifth, the slogan "Black Lives Matter," should be strengthened further to read, "Black Lives Have Value." Racism is imbued in the thinking that Blacks and Whites are not equal, and so is tribalism (that not all tribes are equal). Black lives may matter, but do racists think that Black lives actually, and, in fact, have value? Currently, the experience of many Black people in Europe and America is that Black lives do not have value. This is implicit in the way they are killed or have succumbed to Covid-19. Because most Black people work in relatively less-paying but highly demanded jobs, such as janitors, nurses, social workers, Personal Support Workers (PSWs) and so on, they are also the people who are essential during the Covid-19 pandemic. They may die first. But importantly, too, Blacks are disproportionately poor, live in crowded neighborhoods, may not have access to sound healthcare, may not have insurance coverage, are underpaid, have smaller spaces for social distancing and may not afford masks. This disparity also means that Blacks are the first to contract diseases, and to die from such diseases. This has its basis in the unequal history which has buffeted Blacks for centuries. Blacks, Black Africans, and Black Americans have value. Blacks are humans. They are not animals. They feel pain. They have liberties. They are to be treated with dignity and consideration. They are equal to other humans on earth. They should be treated as such.

And sixth, racism and tribalism cannot be demolished without undoing the unequal disparities that exist in race and tribal relations. There has been protests worldwide fighting to end racism. If racism is ended, so what? The mistake we all make is that we equate racism to a concrete and tangible phenomenon. Racism is not just a social issue, either; racism or tribalism are matters of the heart. By merely saying that, "I am not a racist," it does not mean that I may not be a racist or a tribalist. As Jesus once said, "You will know them by their fruits...."

Racism and tribalism are conceived in the heart, and they ooze from there to manifest socially. And it manifests itself in things people do or omit to do, the policies authorities make or omit to make, and etc. Inequalities are social problems and tackling inequalities may lead to solving the social problem. A good example is when you have an unruly child who wants to do mischief. You can't control the child by simply commanding them to stop being mischievous. You have to do certain things. You may have to give them something or take something away. In other words, you have to regulate the naughty behavior by sanctions or through education. At the national level, racial inequalities can be curbed in the same way.

Education is the long-term cure to inequalities, poverty, and racial injustice. Any other way is simply a quick fix and have no permanent results. It begins at the curriculum level. People should be exposed to matters of equality through education at the very basic level. This is true of the West, and true also of Africa. A curriculum that addresses this deliberately is the long-term solution to issues of inequalities. When children learn that all people are created equal and continue to get responses that validate that sanctity, they will not turn from it when they grow up. A wise sage once said, "Train up a child in the way he should go; even when he is old, he will not depart from it."[56]

If you train children that racism is wrong, they will believe and eventually showcase that ideal in the marketplace of ideas. Instilling anti-racists behavior in children today, means a free and equal society tomorrow. Teaching the children of today that racism offends others and is wrong, means that they will grow into responsible leaders tomorrow.

In USA, most of Western Europe and South Africa, children grew up seeing their parents mistreating Black people; they saw segregated billboards, and they experienced how their parents discriminated against Blacks. So, they also grew up racists and xenophobes. The USA is founded on a land it grabbed from first nations (Aboriginal) people, and on the slave labor and mistreatment inflicted on Black people. It will take deliberate education to erase such historical indignities.

---

[56] Prov. 22:6

Africa must put in its curriculum that it is equal to everyone else in the world, and that it has a responsibility to developing its own land and economy, and not to leaving it to outsiders or "selling" it's best to corporate poachers, just like its fore-parents sold the bravest warriors to the slavers or its political leaders sold its means of production to foreign corporate interests.

Regulation and legislation are the next best solutions to curbing disparities and ending racism. Nations must legislate against inequalities. People must be empowered to live free from discrimination. Differences should be seen as positive factors and not negative weaknesses. Where applicable, some rights must be retroacted to cure or remedy historical wrongs. For example, Canada has entrenched into its Constitution section 15 (2) of the *Charter of Rights and Freedoms* what is known as positive discrimination or Affirmative Action. In essence, in Canada, the government can enact laws that discriminate against the equality of dominant groups in order to offset an historical injustice.

Various provincial legislations also proscribe against the treatment of others based on numerated grounds, including race, national origin or ancestry. Other countries should follow suit. Africa must also enact strong laws that curb inequalities based on tribalism and racism. While legislation may not end racism, it limits those with racist instincts. In short, legislation creates a protective buffer and provides an atmosphere in which racially charged behaviors or tendencies are neutralized.

Against police brutality, for instance, governments can make policies and enact laws that require and compare whether for the same offence, Black people and White people have been treated similarly. And such same laws or policies should prescribe strong remedial and corrective measures to those who may be found culpable. In presenting such legislations, nations should also strengthen equality and diversity in both police enforcement and judicial systems. Even if good laws have been enacted, but if the systems are still White-dominated or are absent of diversity, Black people will still be seen as *clients* of the systems and not equal partners in the implementation and management of the laws. In other words, Blacks will only be *victims*, while their White counterparts will behave as if they exist to police the Blacks, just as the regimes under slavery and Colonialism engendered. If the system is unequal, no matter who occupies the helm, it will still produce unequal, racist and racially-biased outcomes. Policy and legislative changes should also ensure that everyone plays by the same rules. In the USA, for example, the legal and law enforcement apparatuses, dominated by Whites and anchored in strong racists police associations, do not ensure justice for victims of police brutality. The threshold is so high that it is next to impossible to convict a police officer.

Before I delve into discussing the future of Africa in the post-Covid-19 world, it is important that I make a causal nexus between the recent global protests against police brutality and the pandemic. The pandemic revealed the gaping disparities that exist across racial lines. More Blacks in North America and Europe have died from Covid-19 than Whites. Similarly, the protests have also demonstrated that both Whites and Blacks understand the disparities that exist cross racial lines. The biggest threat to the world order is, therefore, not the pandemic, but the historical inequalities that have made Blacks exist as secondary citizens in the world. As it will be argued, many have predicted that despite Africa not having been impacted worse *per capita* like North America and Europe, Africa will still suffer the after-effects of the pandemic as most rich countries will focus on healing their economies. In one sentence, the future of post-Covid-19 Africa is: End the age of dependence and become economically self-sufficient, while combating the gaping social/tribal inequalities.

African Future in a Post-Covid-19 World

Having belabored arguments for a strong education and legislative regime that curbs inequalities in both modern Europe and America and historical Africa, I now move on to discussing the future of Africa in a post-Covid-19 world. I wish to accomplish this thesis by laying out three major points: Africa must not ignore the apathy it received from Western leaders during the Covid-19 pandemic; Africa must not look to the West for leadership, but within itself; and African governments must recruit raw talents scattered abroad.

The UN Secretary General, Antonio Guterres, admitted, March 27th, 2020, on BBC that we are no longer living in a unipolar, bipolar or multipolar world. We are living in a "chaotic" world, controlled by the whims of the USA and the vagaries of China. Donald Trump, for example, had characterized Black African countries as "shitholes." He had also labelled the coronavirus, a "Chinese virus," while China had entertained notions that the virus had its genesis in the Department of Defence (DOD) of the USA. Russia, on the other hand, lurks in the concourses wishing to pounce on the continuously deteriorating relations between the USA and China. This is while Europe is at the blink of an economic devastation brought about by the complete shutting off of the industrial machines in Italy, disillusionment in Spain, finger-pointing in England, and total confusion in France.

As Europe and America are paralyzed, one wonders what would become of Africa, should the pandemic find its ugly claws there, in a post-Covid-19 era. In Europe and America, prior strong economies necessitated the enactment of multi-billion stimulus/rescue packages which acted as a cushion on the ravages of COVID-19. In China, India, Japan and mostly closed Eastern-Asian nations, hegemony and homogeneity had proven assets in pandemic times. Africa lacks both strong economies and homogeneous hegemony.

Post-Covid-19 Africa faces insurmountable challenges at both the healthcare and economic fronts. Already, poverty, seclusionism and tribalism, continue to be self-defeatist menaces against Africa. Covid-19 cannot be allowed to "invade" Africa posthumously, even if a vaccine is available. But it will, sadly, do, if Africa does nothing or continues to play by the same old rules.

Western Apathy towards Africa during Covid-19 and Vaccine Distribution Process

The Covid-19 pandemic has revealed that self-interest still governs relations between Africa and the developed world. Africa is only important if it has a tangible benefit to Western causes. When that cause is redundant or does not rise to the level of creating profit or does not advance Western agendas, Africa is forgotten and even discarded. Canada and other developed formations are exception to this rule. However, for the majority, during the Covid-19 pandemic, fiscal assistance for Africa sank to near zero.

The commonest mantra relished by foreign governments and citizens was that they could not save Africa when their own house was on Covid fire. The *Guardian* reported:

> The Gleneagles deal wasn't perfect but it marked a high point in international cooperation. At a time when the big, developed nations can't even agree a collective response to the Covid-19 pandemic among themselves, it all seems a long time ago. The comparison between the financial firepower being deployed in developed nations and the low-income countries of sub-Saharan Africa is stark. The US Congress has just voted for a $2tn stimulus package. The UK has had four big budget announcements in little more than two weeks. The eurozone has abandoned fiscal austerity and embraced a "whatever it takes" approach. By contrast, Africa is living off scraps. The World Bank has announced $14bn of financial support; the International Monetary Fund has a war-chest of $10bn available for countries in difficulties through a rapid response fund. The leaders of the two organizations are urging creditor countries to suspend debt repayments so that the poorest countries can spend more on health systems.

Prevention is the only remedy Africa has. If Africa must relax and let the virus take root, there will be more untold death and suffering than what is transpired in Italy and Spain. For one, Africa lacks not only medical equipment like ventilators, but masks also and surgical gowns and so on; Africa is ill-equipped to providing basic care to mild symptoms. Unlike in economic terms when the West come to Africa's aid because their situations are more tenable, in this situation, however, it is not likely that the West will be available to help Africa when Western nations themselves face insurmountable challenges with mushrooming coronavirus in their formations.

As inconveniencing as this truth is, it is true, nevertheless. Here are some things African governments must do before and in anticipation of future pandemics.

First, and foremost, "Prevention is far better than cure." There will be no chance for Africa to fight the pandemic. Prevention is the most affordable and reasonable remedy under the circumstance. Africa lacks the medical or otherwise the capacity to fight the pandemic of the scale of Covid-19. Stringent measures unknown in the history of Africa must be taken now. In future, swift actions like closing boarders to contain influenza-like illnesses (ili) must be taken. Critical to the survival of ili is the creation of national stockpiles and revamping of medical facilities and personnel. Covid-19 pandemic has shown that the West are not willing to help Africa when they are themselves going through the same challenges. Africa must stop to rely on Western philanthropy and look within itself to creating conditions for economic emancipation.

Second, everything in government coffers must be spent to provide relief to people as their lives literally come to an end. Africa should not take advantage of these perilous times to only exempt on taxes – Africa must go further and provide money for the citizens to spend, as their lives came to a halt. This is both a challenge and an opportunity. A challenge because Africa has a large percentage of its people poor, uneducated and unemployed. An opportunity – because hitherto, Africa has not taken ambitious strides to providing hope to their struggling populations through economic equalization programs. The end of the pandemic calls for a revolutionary phase in the safe evolution of its societies by being capable of handling its own economic challenges.

And third, Africa must strongly lobby both multilaterals and bilateral communities to completely forgive debt. There is no other way Africa will brave future and similarly-situated pandemics or the Covid-19 aftermath. Seeking for external debt forgiveness is a prudent way of managing the post-Covid-19 pandemic because it ensures that Africa has available resources to allocate to needy areas. The West and monetary organizations must accept this as altruism on their part. This benevolence on the West and monetary organizations' part will be an investment in their future. There is no guarantee that the rich countries will continue to be rich without the help of other nations in the post-Covid-19 era. Strengthening Africa now by means of complete debt forgiveness will create viable avenues for equitable trade later.

Africa Must not Only Look to the West for Leadership but within Itself

African governments must learn to lead themselves. In the past, African leaders first waited to see what their Western or Eastern counterparts would do before they acted. Before Covid-19, African leadership had been more reactionary than visionary. This state of affairs informs why technological, legal, economic and even political changes first have to happen in the West, then the East and last in Africa. This is time for African leadership to become creative, empirical, sophisticated and versatile in ensuring that they fashion culturally-tilted, locally-crafted and provide relevant solutions to real African problems. Africa can no longer wait for Europe or America or the East to lead – Africa must lead itself.

There is attractiveness in chaos – because beauty is the only solution. Covid-19 was a watershed moment. It showed that even Western formations are not ready to fight pandemic of the Covid-19 size. They were caught unawares. They lost many lives, sadly, due to not being prepared to fight the pandemic, especially in Europe and the USA. But Covid-19 also revealed the fact that when a nation is prepared beforehand, it stands a better chance to weather any health or economic forces that may come its way. There were countries in Africa who acted quickly and swiftly to close borders, institute social distance measures and provide masks to their citizenry, and those countries faired relatives well during the pandemic.

In short, Africa considered Covid-19 as a declaration of war. In the similar vein, Africa can marshal its scarce resources, prepare in advance and mobilize its citizens to fight pandemics like inequalities, poverty and corruption. It is possible that Africa can achieve zero corruption, zero poverty, zero disease and zero undemocratic tendencies. It is unlikely that it can reach this milestone depending and relying entirely on Western aid.

African Governments Must Recruit Raw Talents Scattered Abroad

The time has come for Africa to tap into its potential scattered abroad in developed countries. During the 1960s, it was mainly the African students abroad who brought awareness to the idea of independence. Many of those Africans who were educated abroad returned to

Africa to become its first leaders after independence, leaders like Kwame Nkrumah, Jomo Kenyatta, Hastings Kamuzu Banda, and etc. There are many African-born, educated people in the developed countries. These Africans have been exposed to technology, democracy, sustainable healthcare and other system. As noted above, many of them have not realized their potential in the West because of systemic racism and inequalities that exist there.

The Covid-19 pandemic has shown that when nations are locked up, help can only come from within. Africa must, therefore, develop its own people. It can do so safely and cheaply by recruiting the talents in its people abroad. This may call for change of mindset, whereby those Africans in Africa start to see their brothers and sisters abroad as partners in development, and not as competitions for the scarce resources in Africa. This change of attitude will necessitate an exchange of skillsets, experiences and expertise urgently needed to develop Africa.

Africa, too, must start to modernize and modify laws to allow for dual citizens to manage important African government offices, including presidencies. Before Covid-19, most countries in Africa feared that dual citizens would not be patriotic enough to defend Africa. However, the Covid-19 has shown that when nations were faced with a challenge of the scale of Covid-19, they relied on emergency legislations, including relaxing rules that fast-track citizenry in order to provide necessary services to the people. As a proactive step, Africa must return and reintegrate some of its people in important decision-making positions to help reshape the future of Africa. This is nothing new. Africa did the same in 1960s. Benjamin Netanyahu, former Prime Minister of Israel, spent years studying and working in the USA, and went on to be the longest-serving, and probably, the greatest Israeli leader, and had helped to liberalize and develop the Israeli economic frontiers. Africa should do the same.

Conclusion

The post-Covid19 Africa should be a revolutionary Africa. An Africa that is ready to harness its people's talents, at home and abroad, to build an Africa ready to fight for its dominant place in the community of nations. The time for an Africa that is diseased, ill-prepared, begging for existence and devoid of solving its own problems, ended when the nations of the world locked themselves up from the ravages of the injurious Covid-19 pandemic. Devastative as the pandemic was, it also revealed that inequalities, fueled by racism, continue to clobber the global citizens. This thesis has provided the interlinkage between racial inequalities and Covid-19, and in post-Covid-19 world, Africa must play it smart – strive to be equal, end the age of dependence and become economically self-sufficient.

ABOUT THE AUTHOR

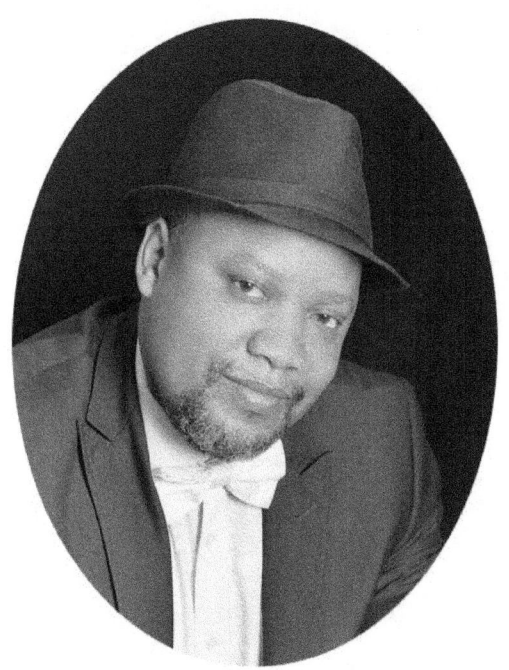

Charles Mwewa (LLB. BA. Education. BA. Legal Studies. Cert. Law. DIBM. LLM Cand.) is a Dad, author, lawyer, educator, and moral and social influencer. Mwewa is the author of 30 books and counting in all genres – fiction (novels), non-fiction and poetry. Mwewa, his wife, and their three girls, reside in the Capital City of Ottawa, Canada.

AUTHOR'S CONTACT

Email address:

spynovel2016@gmail.com

Facebook:

www.facebook.com/charlesmwewa

Twitter:

https://twitter.com/BooksMwewa

Instagram:

instagram.com/mwewabooks/?hl=en

Author's website:

https://www.charlesmwewa.com

To order this book online:

https://www.amazon.com/dp/1988251524

INDEX

3

30-10-60 economic model, 24
30-10-60 Theory, 24

5

500 Fortune, 144

6

666, 128

A

Abomination that Causes Desolation, 128
Abraham, 109
abroad, 2, 4, 40, 42, 44, 47, 48, 49, 50, 52, 153, 158, 159, 160
abuse of power, 119
abuse of resources, 16, 18
academia, 40, 142
Acemoglu, 30, 35
administration, 1, 64
advocacy, 71
advocate, 16, 46
affairs, 2, 19, 31, 75, 78, 122, 157
Affirmative Action, 151
Afghanistan, 87
African National Congress, 89
African scholars, 47
African Union, 82, 90
Afropositive, 125
agendas, 40, 41, 118, 154

agriculture, 24
aid, 17, 136, 155, 158
airport, 50
Alabama, 108
Albania, 45
al-Bashir, 85, 86, 87
alienophobia, 89
ANC, 89
ancestry, 151
Anderson Mazoka, 2
animals, 98, 104, 149
anti-abortion, 123
anti-same-sex, 123
Apartheid, 89, 90
apology, 92
article, 1, 5, 9, 43, 44, 75, 142
associations, 152
atrocities, 80, 84, 90
attend UN Global Food Summit. The Food and Agriculture Organization of the United Nations, 73
AU, 82, 86, 87, 90
Australia, 45, 75
authoritarians, 123
authority, 94, 112, 119, 132
authors, 44, 99

B

Babylon, 121
bacteria, 101
Ban Ki Moon, 14
Bangladesh, 45
Barack Obama, 80, 115, 116, 143
Barak Obama, 111
Barbados, 45

165

BBC, 3, 77, 153
beauty, 102, 103, 111, 158
Belgium, 45
Bembas, 9
Benjamin Netanyahu, 159
Berlin Wall, 69, 93
Bible, 98, 99, 123, 128, 130, 137
bipolar, 153
birth, 34, 50, 69, 101, 125, 127
Black, 53, 75, 89, 90, 97, 104, 105, 106, 108, 113, 114, 115, 125, 141, 142, 143, 144, 145, 146, 148, 150, 151, 153
Black Lives Have Value, 148
Black slave, 97, 147
Blackman, 143
Blake, 99
blessings, 48, 123
Bloody Sunday, 108
Bolshevik Party, 69
bondage, 96, 109
borders, 158
Boris Johnson, 119
brain drain, 49
Brain Earn, 49
breadbasket, 74
Bretton Woods, 32
Britain, 30, 75, 76, 77, 105, 106, 144
brotherhood, 20
brutality, 89, 151, 152
budgets, 131
Bulgaria, 45
Burma, 85
Burundi, 35
Bush, 84, 113

C

C.I.A, 33
Cabinet, 3
Caleb Fundanga, 17
campaign, 55, 66, 115
campaigner, 118
Canada, 2, 6, 8, 19, 21, 22, 23, 36, 39, 45, 47, 50, 52, 80, 105, 106, 107, 116, 118, 125, 126, 141, 151, 154
cancer, 18, 36
candidates, 11, 12, 54, 56
Cantonese, 100
capital, 5, 24, 37, 73, 99, 144, 145
caucus, 35
Cecil Rhodes, 76
Central African Republic, 35
cervix, 128
Chad, 85
Chalwe Mchenga, 62
chambers, 118
chaotic, 153
charges, 146
charismatic, 7
charities, 132
Chaucer, 99
chiefdom, 30
chiefs, 30, 31, 143
children, 19, 35, 64, 75, 103, 109, 110, 146, 150
Chile, 26, 45
China, 45, 47, 71, 84, 86, 93, 94, 95, 153, 154
Chinsali, 10
Christ, 110, 123, 128, 133
Christian, 65, 123
Christian Nation, 65
Chuma, 97
Church, 110, 123
civil society, 35, 71
Civil Society for Poverty Reduction, 16
civil wars, 35, 82
civilizations, 142
Clarice, 107
clergy, 133
clerk, 105
CNN, 77, 80, 107
Cold War, 69

colonial, 14, 15, 30, 47, 55, 78, 98, 105, 145, 147
colonialism, 15, 25, 47, 94, 97, 101, 104, 106, 108, 143, 145, 152
colonists, 97
color, 54, 58, 103, 110, 116, 141, 142, 146
combatants, 82
commander-in-chief, 93
commerce, 142
communalism, 136
Communism, 68
Communist governments, 68
communities, 146, 157
competence, 106
competitions, 159
conflict resolution, 85
Congo DR, 35
congregation, 129, 136, 137
Congress, 143, 155
conscience, 95
conspiracy, 141, 143
Constitution Bill, 51
continent, 17, 31, 81, 87, 125, 142
co-operating partners, 17
cooperation, 73, 74, 139, 140, 155
coordination, 139, 140
copper, 15, 24, 33, 34, 37
coronavirus, 135, 136, 153, 156
corrupt-free culture, 28
corruption, 1, 3, 7, 8, 17, 24, 27, 37, 57, 63, 89, 123, 124, 158
Costa, 26, 45
Covenant of the League of Nations, 105
Covid-19, 5, 127, 128, 129, 130, 132, 133, 134, 136, 137, 138, 139, 141, 148, 152, 153, 154, 155, 156, 157, 158, 159, 160
Covid-19 pandemic, 5, 129, 137, 148, 153, 154, 155, 156, 157, 159, 160
created equal, 143, 150
Creator, 143

crime, 147
crisis, 86, 139
Croatia, 45
CSPR, 16
culture, 22, 36, 50, 70, 72, 78, 101, 102, 103, 106, 115, 146
curriculum, 150, 151
Cyprus, 45
Czarist regime, 69
Czech Republic, 45

D

Dan Brown, 99
Daniel, 128
Darfur, 5, 80, 85, 86, 87, 88
David Livingstone, 97
death, 34, 101, 109, 110, 133, 155
decentralize power, 71
decision, 76, 117, 118, 119, 120, 140, 159
decisions, 20, 62, 118
decolonization, 69
demagoguism, 122
democracy, 2, 3, 14, 28, 67, 68, 69, 70, 71, 72, 93, 95, 118, 119, 125, 159
democratic institutions, 7, 14, 30
democratic society, 53, 70
democratization, 14, 69
demon, 64
Department of Defence, 153
Derek Chauvin, 148
descendants, 109, 145
developed country, 2, 41, 49, 52
dialects, 100
diaspora, 4, 5, 19
dignity, 18, 77, 116, 125, 146, 148, 149
dilation, 127
Director of Public Prosecution, 61
discipline, 7, 45, 142
discrimination, 91, 108, 113, 116, 126, 151

disease, 32, 37, 80, 83, 85, 128, 129, 136, 158
disparities, 5, 149, 151, 152
distribution, 5, 140, 146
District Commissioners, 105
diversity, 152
DOD, 153
Don Cheadle, 81
Don't Kubeba, 8
donor aid, 14, 16
DPP, 61, 62, 63, 65
dream, 25, 44, 110, 116, 126
dual citizens, 4, 47, 159
dual citizenship, 43, 44, 45, 46, 50, 51
Durban, 92

E

economic liberalism, 16
economies, 68, 94, 153, 154
economy, 5, 14, 20, 23, 24, 27, 32, 33, 55, 56, 68, 71, 76, 145, 151
Edgar Lungu, 1, 7, 59
education, 5, 19, 32, 45, 47, 48, 50, 70, 102, 142, 145, 147, 150, 153
Edward Colston, 144
effacement, 127
Egypt, 45, 109, 112
election, 1, 2, 8, 10, 53, 54, 55, 59, 64, 68, 86, 90, 108, 113, 123
elections, 4, 14, 15, 16, 30, 46, 54, 55, 56, 60, 62, 71, 72, 77, 89, 108, 113
Electoral College, 113
Electoral Commission of Zambia, 113
electoral fairness, 70
email, 131
emancipation, 69, 156
emergency orders, 118
emergency powers, 139
Emerging African Leadership, 70, 72
Emmerance, 107
empires, 121

employer, 55
employment, 45, 71, 89, 137
encourage, 30, 101, 133
endurance, 8, 116
Engels, 68
engineer, 1
Enoch Kavindele, 44
equal partners, 152
equality, 68, 70, 105, 110, 116, 145, 150, 151, 152
equalization, 95, 125, 156
equilibrium, 94
Eric Chanda, 43
Eritrea, 35
Euro Crisis, 16
Europe, 16, 24, 26, 36, 47, 75, 80, 86, 87, 128, 141, 142, 144, 145, 148, 150, 152, 153, 154, 158
European Union, 73, 80
Europeans, 97, 101, 145
Evangelical, 121, 122
evil, 84, 96, 101, 122
extinction, 104

F

fairness, 113
famine, 37, 127
FAO, 73
favor, 54, 71, 112, 113
FDI, 48
fertile, 36, 144
fertilizer, 23, 58
Finland, 45
Florida, 108
food, 13, 19, 23, 73, 111, 131
forefathers, 146
foreign, 33, 48, 98, 151, 155
foreign investment, 33
foreign-driven development, 33
foreigners, 43, 77, 89, 90, 91, 92
forgiveness, 123, 157

Fox News, 144
France, 45, 154
Frederick Chiluba, 1, 9, 16, 62
free and fair, 14, 30, 72
freedom, 14, 19, 20, 22, 24, 27, 30, 44, 46, 69, 94, 96, 111, 122
freedoms, 14, 64, 70, 91
free-market competition, 16
free-market economy, 71
French, 100
FTJ, 3
fundamental human rights, 14, 70

G

Gaza, 87
GDP, 23, 24, 32, 33
General Williams Carter Wickham, 144
genocide, 80, 81, 82, 85, 86, 87, 88, 90
George Floyd, 144, 148
Germany, 45
global economic leader, 25
globalization, 45, 51
God, 59, 65, 80, 81, 88, 109, 110, 114, 123, 129, 130, 131, 132, 133, 137, 138
gold-standard, 96
Gospel, 128, 131, 133, 134
governance, 4, 14, 16, 26, 30, 49, 119, 122
governed, 20, 31, 32, 63
Governor General, 125
governors, 32
Greece, 45, 121
Guerilla warfare, 85
Guy Scot, 55, 58

H

H1N1, 5, 79, 87
habitation, 31
haciendas, 144

happiness, 24, 26, 143
harmony, 10
Hastings Kamuzu Banda, 159
healing, 65, 153
health, 35, 83, 136, 137, 155, 158
healthcare, 5, 136, 146, 149, 154, 159
hegemony, 154
HH, 1, 2, 4, 5, 7, 8, 9, 10, 11, 12
Hichilema, 1, 2, 10, 59
Highly Indebted Poor Country Initiative, 33
history, 10, 12, 25, 30, 40, 67, 68, 84, 86, 89, 104, 108, 109, 111, 112, 113, 114, 115, 126, 142, 146, 156
HIV/AIDS, 34, 75
Hollywood, 103
homeland, 51
homelessness, 19
hooligans, 90
hospitals, 13, 37, 136
house, 53, 105, 107, 155
human rights violation, 83
humanitarian emergencies, 82
humanity, 86, 87, 101, 103, 104, 105, 106, 108, 112, 144, 148
Hungary, 45
Hutus, 81, 84
hypocrisy, 85, 122

I

ICC, 86
Iceland, 45
ICISS, 82
identification, 50
ideological polarity, 25
ideology, 27, 68
ili, 156
illiteracy, 99
IMF, 32, 148
immigrants, 122, 145
immigration, 49

immunity, 61, 63
imperialist, 76
imprisonments, 108
incarcerations, 146
incompetence, 142
independence, 9, 15, 17, 40, 47, 75, 97, 106, 147, 158
India, 31, 45, 50, 67, 154
indictment, 86
Indirect Rule, 31
Industrial Revolution, 104
industrialized countries, 71
industry, 33, 36, 40, 49, 103
inequalities, 27, 142, 143, 146, 147, 149, 150, 151, 152, 153, 158, 159, 160
infection, 137
infections, 101
influence, 20, 113, 122
influenza-like illnesses, 156
information, 80, 140
infrastructure, 3, 13, 31, 37, 142, 146
injustice, 106, 141, 145, 150, 151
insurance, 149
integrity, 63, 122
intellectual, 24, 105, 106
intelligence, 138
International Commission on Intervention and State Sovereignty, 82
international community, 20, 82, 85, 86, 87
International Criminal Court, 86
International Financial Institutions, 16
International Monetary Fund, 148, 155
Internet, 104
interpretation, 128
intolerances, 91
investment opportunities, 44
IQ, 99
Iraq, 76, 84, 87
Iron Curtain, 93

Isaac, 109
Israel, 45, 50, 109, 159
Israelites, 109, 110
Italy, 45, 154, 155

J

Jacob, 89, 109
Jacob Zuma, 89
Jamaica, 45
James Bevel, 108
Janjaweed, 85
JEM, 85
Jerusalem, 128
Jesus, 122, 129, 149
Jews, 50, 104, 129
Jim Anderson, 74
jobs, 5, 27, 37, 45, 46, 51, 53, 55, 56, 91, 133, 145, 148
Johannesburg, 91
Jomo Kenyatta, 159
Joseph, 109, 112
Joshua, 110
journalist, 19, 115
Judas, 59
judicial activism, 119
junta, 85
justice, 61, 66, 86, 87, 104, 123, 142, 152
Justice and Equality Movement, 85
Justice Mambilima, 64

K

Karl Marx, 68
Kelvin Chitala, 17
Kenneth Kaunda, 1, 9, 16, 32, 62
Kenya, 67, 70, 72
kingdom, 123, 127
KK, 3, 9, 10, 54
Kosovo, 45, 83, 84, 87
Kwame Nkrumah, 159

Kwerekweres, 89

L

labor, 20, 31, 99, 104, 109, 128, 144, 150
Lady Brenda Hale, 117
lands, 50, 68, 104
language, 98, 99, 100, 145
Larry King Live, 80
LAS, 86
Last Woe, 128
Latvia, 45
law, 1, 8, 39, 46, 62, 64, 65, 70, 76, 90, 92, 105, 117, 118, 119, 123, 132, 133, 142, 146, 152
law-enforcement, 142
lawyer, 62, 145
lawyers, 146
leadership, 28, 47, 48, 53, 54, 64, 70, 72, 78, 106, 123, 139, 141, 143, 153, 157
League of Arab States, 86
legacy, 11, 66, 98
legislation, 46, 106, 140, 151
legitimate power, 65
Lenin, 69
Levy Mwanawasa, 1, 9, 16
liability, 65, 142
liberalism, 20
Liberals, 73
Liberia, 35
liberties, 45, 149
liberty, 68, 143
life, 8, 22, 24, 27, 40, 41, 43, 44, 45, 46, 62, 94, 95, 96, 101, 102, 110, 111, 143, 145, 148
limited governance, 20
living standard, 13
lobby, 71, 157
Louisiana, 116
lower-class, 26, 27

Lozi, 100
Lozis, 10, 12
Luapula, 1
Luis Moreno-Ocampo, 86
Lusaka, 13, 22, 31, 32, 89
Luvale, 100

M

Macbeth, 53
Madagascar, 35
Magna Carta, 120
Mainza Chona, 10
majority poor, 14, 17, 37, 53
Malawi, 9, 35
Malta, 45
Mandarin, 100
Mandela, 77, 89, 90, 92, 141
manifesto, 2
Marcos Rodrigues, 17
Margaret Chan, 79
Mark of the Beast, 128
markets, 144
marriage, 101, 123
Martin Luther King, 108, 110, 116, 144
Marxist-Leninism, 69
Marylyn Celli, 16
masks, 136, 149, 155, 158
Mason Temple, 110
Matamela Cyril Ramaphosa, 89
mealie meal, 16, 58
media, 32, 46, 70, 74, 80, 102, 103, 130, 131, 142
Mediterranean Sea, 87
memorandum of understanding (MOU), 106
Memphis, 110
Mexico, 45, 79, 83, 115
Michael Sata, 1, 9, 10, 17, 18, 38, 62
Michaelle Jean, 125
middle-class, 24, 26, 27
Miles Sampa, 59

military, 15, 84, 85, 114, 142
militia, 85
Milupi, 98
minds, 7, 30, 100, 141, 144
mineral, 30, 33
mini-buses, 137
mining, 23, 24, 33, 66
minions, 7
Minneapolis, 144
minority, 122
mistreatment, 141, 142, 150
MOB, 128
money, 3, 48, 122, 123, 131, 133, 137, 141, 156
moral turpitude, 121
Morgan Tsvangirai, 73
Mosi-oa-Tunya Falls, 97
Mount Nebo, 109
mountaintop, 109
movements, 3, 69, 140
Mpezeni, 98
Mugabe, 67, 70, 73, 74, 75, 76, 77, 78, 94
Mulla, 13, 14
multiparty, 3, 69
multipolar, 153
murder, 144
Mutembo Nchito, 61, 62, 63
Mwai Kibaki, 67, 68
Mwansa, 98
Myanmar, 85

N

NAM, 86
national stockpiles, 156
nationalism, 20
nationalist, 70
natives, 31
NATO, 81, 84
Nazism, 70
Ndhlovus, 98

neglect of industries, 16, 18
neo-colonial, 33
Neo-Colonialism, 101
Neo-Patrimonialism, 58
Nevers Mumba, 54, 59
new government, 3, 59, 69
New World, 109
New Zealand, 75
Newton Ng'uni, 64
NGOs, 71, 132
Niger, 35
Nigeria, 15, 22, 50, 94
Nile Delta, 36
nomination, 59, 116
Non-Aligned Movement, 86
non-Blacks, 142
Non-Governmental Organizations, 71
North America, 75, 87, 142, 152
North Atlantic Treaty Organization, 81
Northern Hemisphere, 83
Northern Rhodesia, 105
nuclear, 99
Nyanja, 9, 12, 53, 56, 100

O

OAU, 90
Obamagate, 143
October Revolution, 69
office, 8, 47, 54, 63, 65, 71, 107, 115, 119
OHRC, 106
OMS Rule, 94, 95
One-Man Strong Rule, 94
One-Party State, 63
Ontario, 23, 39, 106
opposition, 35, 59, 73, 95
orators, 100
outbreak, 79, 87, 88, 127, 128, 139

P

Pacific, 142
pains, 116, 127
Pakistan, 45, 87
Panama, 26, 45
pandemic, 34, 80, 129, 130, 131, 135, 136, 137, 139, 152, 154, 156, 158, 160
parastatal, 63
Parliament, 61, 118, 119
parliamentarians, 51
passports, 50
pastor, 129
patriotism, 20, 40
peace, 10, 26, 51, 81, 82, 83, 84
peacekeepers, 84
peacekeeping, 81, 82, 84, 86
peacemakers, 84
Peel Regional Police, 106
penitence, 65
People's Liberation Army, 85
Personal Protective Equipment, 136
Personal Support Workers, 148
Peru, 31, 45
pestilences, 127
Peter, 112, 133
PF, 1, 8, 12, 59, 62, 63, 64
Pharaoh, 109
philanthropy, 156
Philippines, 45
philosophy, 32
Phiris, 98
physicians, 129, 136
Pierre Berton, 19
Pisgah, 109
planet, 126
plantations, 144
plunderism, 78
poachers, 151
poison, 129, 137
police, 64, 91, 108, 141, 144, 146, 148, 151, 152
policies, 1, 7, 35, 36, 41, 69, 74, 95, 106, 149, 151
policy implementation, 3
political parties, 35, 54, 86, 115
politician, 40, 123
politicians, 10, 12, 31, 34, 41, 61, 65, 117, 118, 119, 123
politicization of society, 70
politics, 1, 2, 7, 9, 10, 11, 32, 40, 46, 48, 56, 57, 61, 63, 64, 65, 69, 78, 95, 100, 102, 107, 123, 142
popular vote, 113
population, 5, 13, 20, 23, 26, 27, 28, 31, 34, 146, 147
portfolios, 5
Portugal, 45
Portuguese Revolution, 69
post-Covid-19 Africa, 153
poverty, 1, 5, 7, 8, 14, 15, 16, 17, 18, 20, 22, 30, 34, 35, 37, 60, 64, 72, 75, 89, 141, 147, 150, 154, 158
poverty reduction programs, 14, 16
power-hungry, 58, 113
PPE, 136
prayers, 133
preach, 130, 133
pregnant, 127
prejudice, 115, 116, 126
Prevention is far better than cure, 156
pride, 116
priests, 137
Prime Minister, 85, 119, 125, 159
primitive, 101
privileges, 47, 120
productivity, 27, 30, 36
professionals, 131
professor, 21
progress, 7, 33, 42, 46, 52, 62, 67, 70, 77, 113, 125, 140
Promised Land, 109, 110, 111
property, 37, 49, 68, 85, 104, 144, 146

prorogation, 118, 119
prorogue, 119
prosperity, 17, 26, 40, 46
protests, 141, 146, 149, 152
provinces, 22, 140
PSWs, 148
public opinion, 9

Q

Queen of England, 119

R

R2P, 82, 83, 85, 90
race, 7, 25, 53, 58, 104, 108, 110, 112, 126, 149, 151
racism, 91, 106, 116, 126, 141, 142, 143, 149, 150, 151, 159, 160
racists, 142, 148, 150, 152
Realists, 74
regimes, 3, 30, 85, 152
Regional Commissioners, 105
regulations, 136
religion, 142
Republic of Zambia, 15, 136
rescue, 131, 154
resources, 3, 13, 22, 24, 30, 33, 48, 55, 58, 59, 81, 83, 99, 144, 146, 157, 158, 159
Responsibility to Protect, 81, 82, 90
revolutions, 68
River Zambezi, 20
Robinson, 30, 35
Romania, 45
Rome, 73, 121
Romeo Dallaire, 81, 84
Rubicon, 58
Rule of a Man, 96
Rule of Law, 61, 63, 95, 118, 119, 122
ruling parties, 65, 118
rumors, 135

Rupiah Banda, 1, 9, 16, 62, 63
Russia, 47, 69, 84, 86, 153
Rwanda, 81, 83, 84, 85, 90

S

sacrifice, 45, 90
sacrifices, 116, 146
Sadiq al-Mahdi, 85
Sahara, 72
saints, 133
salvation, 129
SAPs, 16
saving, 24, 27, 137
savings, 123, 131
Scarborough, 22
schools, 37, 100, 146
scientists, 37, 129
Scriptures, 137
Second Sudanese Civil War, 85
secondary citizens, 152
secularism, 121
Security Council, 84
segregation, 147
self-defence, 82
self-government, 2, 70
self-interest, 83, 87, 154
self-isolation, 129
self-sufficient, 36, 153, 160
Selma to Montgomery, 108
Senator, 115, 116
Serbia, 45
Seven Angels, 128
Seven Plagues, 128
Seventh Trumpet, 128
Shakespeare, 53, 99
shitholes, 106, 153
simple majority, 113
Situation Room, 83
SLA, 85
slavery, 92, 101, 104, 108, 143, 146, 147, 152

Slovenia, 45
social distance, 129, 130, 158
Socialism, 68, 94
Solomon, 111, 112
Somalia, 35
South Africa, 45, 46, 76, 77, 89, 90, 91, 92, 94, 150
South Korea, 45
South-East Asia, 124
sovereign, 22, 69, 70, 76, 82, 83, 84
sovereignty, 76, 78
Spain, 45, 154, 155
Spanish, 100
SPLA, 85
squalors, 37
Sri-Lanka, 87
St. Catharines, 22
St. Paul, 116
Stalinism, 70
State House, 114, 135
stimulus, 131, 154, 155
street vendors, 37
Structural Adjustment Programs, 16
struggle, 15, 108
Struggles of My People, 99
successor, 7, 110
Sudan, 80, 85
Sudanese Liberation Army, 85
Supreme Court, 117
surgical gowns, 155
surplus, 24, 27
Sweden, 45
swine flu, 79, 80, 83
Switzerland, 23, 24, 26, 45
sycophants, 7
symptoms, 16, 18, 155
synergy, 5, 7
Syria, 45

T

talents, 5, 153, 159, 160

Taliban, 87
tax, 66
taxable ventures, 37
technology, 22, 40, 41, 48, 101, 103, 104, 106, 125, 128, 130, 159
temptations, 132
Tennessee, 110
terrorism, 51, 83, 141
terrorists, 74
testimony, 128
Thabo Mbeki, 89, 91
the press, 70
the West, 2, 4, 17, 25, 41, 47, 74, 75, 86, 87, 88, 90, 93, 102, 103, 145, 150, 153, 155, 156, 157, 159
Third World, 47
Tonga, 10, 100
Toronto, 102, 111, 115, 146
trade, 25, 77, 94, 142, 145, 147, 157
traditions, 7
transfer of power, 71
transgression, 133
Treaty of Westphalia, 76
Treehouse, 107
Tribal Balancing, 10
tribal politics, 123
tribalism, 10, 12, 148, 149, 151, 154
tribe, 7, 9, 53, 54, 56, 109
Trump, 3, 94, 95, 106, 121, 122, 123, 143, 153
Trumpism, 124
truth, 41, 71, 75, 77, 82, 89, 105, 111, 116, 123, 125, 126, 130, 156
Turkey, 45
Tutsis, 81, 90
Tyranny of the Majority, 57, 119

U

UFO, 63
Uganda, 94, 95
ugly, 59, 103, 154

UK, 50, 117, 118, 120, 155
UKSC, 117, 118, 119
UN Global Food Summit, 73
unanimous, 117, 118, 120
undemocratic tendencies, 7, 11, 119, 158
unemployed, 37, 111, 156
UNICEF, 35
unipolar, 153
United Kingdom, 45, 75, 94
United Nations Universal Declaration of Human Rights, 91
United Party for National Development, 1
United States, 45, 67, 76, 108, 110, 111, 113, 115, 116, 122, 123, 143
university, 21, 48, 147
University of Zambia, 17, 32
UNZA, 17
UNZA Student Union, 17
UPND, 1, 2
upper-class, 26, 27
US National Historic Trail, 108
USA, 22, 46, 47, 50, 52, 53, 76, 89, 97, 118, 141, 143, 144, 145, 147, 150, 152, 153, 158, 160

V

vaccine, 5, 154
vaccines, 5
vaginal delivery, 128
value, 47, 70, 102, 111, 148
Van Gore, 99
vengeance, 60, 62, 63, 65, 67, 78
ventilators, 136, 155
violence, 90, 91
virus, 101, 133, 153, 155
VISA, 48
visionary leader, 3
voiceless, 71

W

war, 15, 17, 26, 37, 44, 51, 72, 83, 84, 85, 86, 87, 155, 158
weaknesses, 7, 123, 151
wealth, 3, 22, 30, 31, 45, 123, 146, 148
weapon, 65, 98, 143
Western democracies, 3
Western World, 80
Westernism, 41, 101, 102
White Supremacists, 89
WHO, 57, 58, 79, 80
wisdom, 7, 40, 114, 128
Wolf Blitzer, 83
work, 1, 27, 30, 36, 40, 41, 45, 47, 89, 132, 148
world citizenship, 51
World Conference against Racism, Racial Discrimination, Xenophobia and Related Intolerance, 92
worship, 33, 101, 129, 130, 136

X

xenophobes, 150
xenophobia, 77, 89, 91, 92, 113
Xi, 94, 95
Xi Jinping Thought, 94

Y

Yoweri Museveni, 95

Z

Zambianism, 20
zero, 8, 147, 154, 158
Zimbabwe, 35, 67, 68, 70, 72, 73, 74, 75, 76, 77, 94

www.ingramcontent.com/pod-product-compliance
Lightning Source LLC
Chambersburg PA
CBHW051530240526
45471CB00019B/320